IMPROVING YOUR CLOCK REPAIRING SKILLS

IMPROVING YOUR CLOCK REPAIRING SKILLS

Harold C. Kelly

ASSOCIATION PRESS · NEW YORK

HAROLD C. KELLY
is also the author of
Clock Repairing as a Hobby
and
Watch Repairing as a Hobby
in this series

IMPROVING YOUR CLOCK REPAIRING SKILLS
Copyright © 1976 by Harold C. Kelly
Published by Association Press, 291 Broadway, New York, N.Y. 10007

International Standard Book Number: 0–8096–1907–5
Library of Congress Catalog Card Number: 75-42334

Library of Congress Cataloging in Publication Data

Kelly, Harold Caleb.
Improving your clock repairing skills.

Bibliography: p.
Includes index.
1. Clocks and watches—Repairing and adjusting.
I. Title.
TS547.K36   681'.113'028   75-42334
ISBN 0-8096-1907-5

Printed in the United States of America
Designed by The Etheredges

 CONTENTS

6   CONTENTS

 PREFACE

Back in 1971 Robert Roy Wright, Managing Editor of Association Press, suggested that I write a book on clock repair for the beginner—that is, for those who had never taken a look at the clock movement. This was done and my book entitled *Clock Repairing as a Hobby* was published in 1972.

Now it has been suggested that I write a book for those who have passed the beginner's stage—that is, for those who have given a good hard look at the clock movement and now want a book with more advanced material. It is hoped that this book does just that.

The basic theory and design of the regulator clock, the subject of gearing, escapements, and a thorough analysis of the pendulum are given space herein. Of course, the repair and adjustment techniques are treated in detail. It follows that if one studies and repairs clock movements in this manner, he is no longer a beginner. Instead, he becomes a qualified and advanced clock repairer and deserves to be so rated. My best wishes go to those of you who persevere in your efforts to become such qualified and advanced clock repairers.

H.C.K.

 # WHEEL WORK
OF PENDULUM
CLOCKS

Pendulum clocks vary in size, style, and construction as much as do balance wheel timepieces. Tower clocks have pendulums that are 13 or more feet in length and we have seen small novelty clocks in which the pendulum was only 3½ inches long. Obviously these differ in construction. Small clocks are mainspring driven, while many wall clocks are weight driven. Nearly all grandfather clocks are weight driven.

All mechanical clocks require wheels and the parts have special names. The projections around the circumference of a wheel are called *teeth*. The piece that receives the turning pressure from the teeth of the wheel is called a *pinion* and the projections around the circumference of the pinion are called *leaves*.

A number of wheels gearing into pinions and finally reaching the escape wheel constitute what is called the *main train*. Add to this the *escapement* and *pendulum* and we have all that is needed for time control.

In addition to the main train all modern clocks have a second train called the *dial train*. This train controls the movement of the hands. It is analyzed in a later section of this chapter.

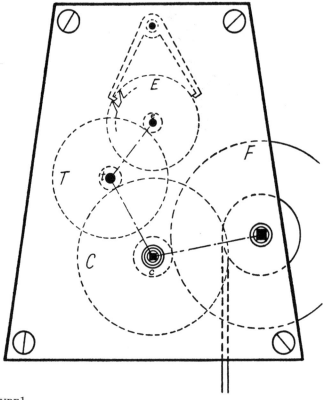

FIGURE 1
Movement of the American regulator clock
F–first wheel
C–second or center wheel   c–second pinion
T–third wheel   t–third pinion
E–escape wheel   e–escape pinion

MAIN TRAIN OF WEIGHT-DRIVEN CLOCKS

For the purpose of describing the main train, let us consider the standard regulator movement. This movement is of the simplest construction, containing only four wheels in the main train, plus, of course, the dial train. It is powered by a weight and is usually fitted with a pendulum beating seconds. In a latitude of 40 degrees, the seconds pendulum is 39.1 inches long. A formula for pendulum length is given on page 49.

Figure 1 shows a regulator movement of the American type. The *first wheel,* sometimes called the *great wheel,* has attached to it a grooved cylinder called a *drum* upon which a metal cable is wound. To the end of the cable is attached the weight. The first wheel drives the second, or center, pinion to which is attached the center wheel. (Note that the second pinion is, in reality, the first pinion, but for convenience it is given the same name as the second, or center, wheel of which it is a part.) The center wheel carries the minute hand and of course makes one turn in an hour. The center wheel drives the third pinion and wheel, which in turn drives the escape pinion and wheel.

CALCULATING THE TURNS OF THE MAIN TRAIN

The formula for the main train in the regulator movement is as follows:

$$\frac{FCT}{cte} = \text{number of turns of the escape wheel}$$

in which the capital letters *FCT* indicate the number of teeth on the first, center and third wheels and the small letters *cte* indicate the number of leaves on the center, third and escape pinions.

Substituting the numerical values we have:

$$\frac{144 \times 96 \times 90}{12 \times 12 \times 12} = 720 \text{ turns of the escape wheel.}$$

CALCULATING THE NUMBER OF BEATS

The escape wheel in the regulator movement must deliver 60 impulses to the pendulum with each turn in order to register seconds. To accomplish this, the escape wheel must have 30 teeth, for each tooth delivers 2 impulses: first to the receiving pallet and second to the discharging pallet.

We will start now with the center wheel, since our formula must show one revolution per hour. Letting E indicate the escape wheel, the formula now reads:

$$\frac{CT \ 2E}{te} = \text{number of beats per hour.}$$

Substituting the numerical values we have:

$$\frac{96 \times 90 \times 2 \times 30}{12 \times 12} = 3600 \text{ beats per hour.}$$

Since the escape wheel makes one turn in a minute, a second hand may be fixed to the extremity of the escape-wheel arbor. This is the usual practice in the construction of regulator clocks. A long pivot on the escape-wheel arbor extends through a hole in the dial and the second hand is fitted by friction.

MAIN TRAIN OF MAINSPRING-DRIVEN CLOCKS

Since pendulum clocks are made in such a large variety of types and sizes, it follows that the main train must sometimes be designed with additional wheels if the proper ratio is to be maintained between the beat of the pendulum and the required speed of the center wheel and the escape wheel. In the formula shown below, a fourth wheel has been added to the main train, and the movement is powered by a mainspring.

$$\frac{\text{CTF2E}}{\text{tfe}} = \text{beats per hour.}$$

Substituting the numerical values:

$$\frac{64 \times 48 \times 40 \times 2 \times 15}{8 \times 8 \times 8} = 7200 \text{ beats per hour.}$$

The above main train uses a pendulum beating half-seconds and its length is 9.78 inches.

POWER UNIT OF MAINSPRING-DRIVEN CLOCKS

There are two types of power systems in use in mainspring-driven clocks.

1. The lower-priced clocks use what is termed an *open spring*—that is, the mainspring is not enclosed in a barrel. The outer end of the mainspring is secured around a pillar that lies between the plates, while the inner end hooks on an arbor that carries the first wheel. A ratchet wheel is attached to the arbor and the click is secured to the first wheel. This is an inexpensive and reliable arrangement, but it has limitations with regard to accuracy. When the mainspring is wound, the power is taken off the train momentarily, causing the clock to lose time. When the winding ceases, the power is again delivered to the first wheel through the ratchet wheel and click and thence to the train.

2. In the better-grade clocks, the mainspring is enclosed in a barrel called the *going barrel*. As is the case with the open mainspring movement, the mainspring is

wound through the arbor. The arbor carries the ratchet, and the click is attached to the plate and the mainspring is wound from the center. But in this type of movement, it is the barrel rather than the arbor which is secured to the first wheel. Since the outer end of the mainspring is attached to the barrel, it follows that the power is always maintained to the train so long as the mainspring is under tension. Mainsprings fitted in going barrels should occupy one-third of the space between the barrel wall and the arbor.

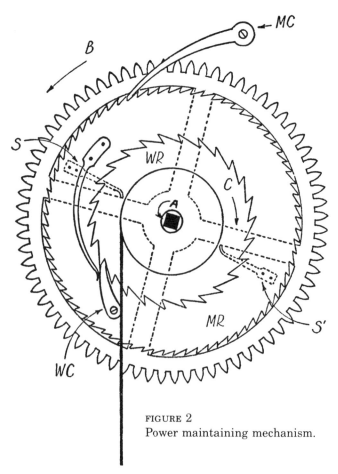

FIGURE 2
Power maintaining mechanism.

POWER MAINTAINING MECHANISM

When a weight-driven clock requires winding, the act of winding tends to reverse the train, possibly jamming the escapement and thus interfering with the timekeeping. A power maintaining device overcomes this difficulty and the clock is kept going. This mechanism, invented by John Harrison in 1745 and still used in clocks of regulator quality, is shown in Figure 2. The winding ratchet wheel *WR* is attached to the drum and both are fixed to the arbor *A*. The maintaining ratchet wheel *MR* lies outside of the winding ratchet wheel and is free to turn on the arbor. Lying next is the first wheel and it, too, is free on the arbor and also free of the maintaining ratchet.

ACTION OF THE MAINTAINING MECHANISM

The winding click *WC* is pivoted to the maintaining ratchet wheel *MR*, and its point engages the teeth of the winding ratchet wheel *WR*. The clock is running by its weight and the two ratchet wheels turn together since click *WC* carries the power to the wheel *MR*. The maintaining springs *S* and *S'* are soon under tension and all parts are now turning in the direction of the arrow *B*. Now, suppose the clock is being wound. The winding ratchet wheel will be turning in the direction of the arrow *C*. The maintaining ratchet is held from turning backwards by the maintaining click *MC*, which is pivoted to the clock plate. The force created by the maintaining springs *S* and *S'* drives the first wheel in the direction of the arrow *B*, thus providing the necessary power to the train as the clock is being wound.

DOUBLE CORD

In order to reduce the fall of the weight without reducing the drum diameter to impractical proportions, it is sometimes desirable to use a double cable as shown in Figure 3. In this case the weight falls only half as fast, but note that twice the weight is required.

THE DIAL TRAIN

Figure 4 shows the dial train of the type used in the regulator clock. This construction is practically the same in all types of clocks. The center wheel, which turns once in an hour, is fitted near the center of the movement and has a long arbor which extends through a hole in the dial. A tube with a pinion at its base, called the *cannon pinion* (C in Figure 4) fits with a slight friction on the center arbor

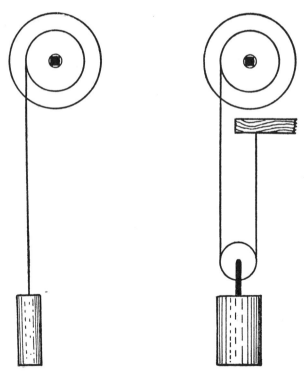

FIGURE 3
Single- and double-cord systems.

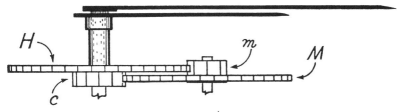

FIGURE 4
Dial train used in the regulator clock.

and turns with it when the clock is running. In setting the hands to time, the entire dial train turns independently of the center arbor. The upper end of the cannon pinion carries the minute hand and the pinion at the base drives the minute wheel M. To the minute wheel is secured the minute pinion m, which in turn drives the hour wheel H. This last wheel fits freely on the cannon pinion and carries the hour hand. The dial train is so designed as to cause the hour hand to make one turn to every twelve turns of the minute hand.

The formula reads as follows, using the letters as given above to indicate the wheels and pinions:

$$\frac{MH}{cm} = 12.$$

Substituting the numerical values:

$$\frac{60 \times 42}{15 \times 14} = 12.$$

The dial train may be formed by many different combinations, the only requirement being that the combined ratios equal 12.

Another function attached to the dial train is found in the rack-and-snail striking clocks. The snail is generally mounted on the pipe of the hour wheel. When assembling the dial train the hour wheel must be fitted in such a manner that the rack drops to the lowest step on the snail. This ensures that the clock will strike correctly.

GEARING

The gearing of a clock is made up of wheels and pinions whose circumferences are covered with teeth and leaves. The function of a tooth is to press on a leaf in such a manner that it will cause the pinion to turn with a velocity that is constant to the wheel. This requires that the wheels have teeth and the pinions have leaves so shaped as to conform to certain scientific principles.

PRINCIPLES OF GEARING

In order to visualize this more clearly, let us assume that there is a circle within the toothed section of the wheel that has a common velocity with a similar circle of the pinion and that these circles touch each other. This would be compared to a roller without teeth driving a smaller roller merely by friction. The circumferences of both rollers would have a common velocity, provided there is no slipping action. In a gearing, these circles are called *pitch circles,* and although their theoretical location is not so clearly defined, they have a real existence, nevertheless. Figure 5 shows the pitch circles cutting through the middle portion of the teeth. That part of a tooth lying outside the pitch circle is called the *addendum.* That part lying inside is called the *dedendum.* When a wheel drives a pinion, it will be observed that the addenda of the wheel teeth act only on the dedenda of the pinion leaves.

EPICYCLOID AND HYPOCYCLOID

The shape of the *addenda* of the wheel teeth most used in clocks and watches is derived from a geometrical curve called the *epicycloid.* This is formed by means of a point on one circle while it is rolling on another circle. Figure 6 shows how the curve is formed. The portion of a circle *A* represents the pitch circle of the wheel. A smaller circle *B* equals half the pitch diameter of the pinion and just touches the pitch circle of the wheel *A.* Let us suppose that circle *B* (called the *generating circle*) was cut out of

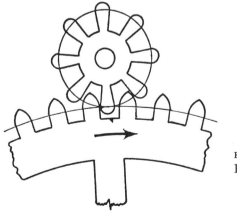

FIGURE 5
Pitch circle.

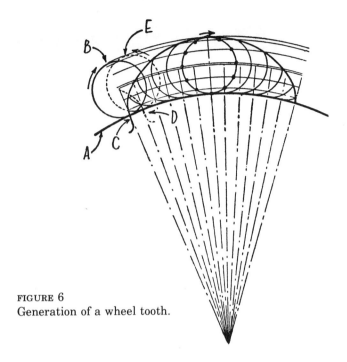

FIGURE 6
Generation of a wheel tooth.

cardboard as was likewise the pitch circle A. Now, place
these circles on a sheet of drawing paper with the generating circle B just touching the circle A, and fit a pencil
marker to the generating circle at the point where the two
circles meet. Next, roll generating circle B on circle A,
without slipping, in the direction of the arrow at top. In so
doing, the pencil point will trace the side of the tooth,
indicated by the line C.

It is observed that the analysis of the epicycloid as
given above takes account of only one side of a tooth. The
question now arises as to how to determine the width of
the tooth. This is found by dividing 360 (the number of
degrees in any circle) by the number of teeth in the wheel.
This gives, in degrees, the width of one tooth and one
space, generally referred to as *circular pitch*.

Thus $\dfrac{360 \text{ degrees}}{80 \text{ teeth}} = 4.5$ degrees of circular pitch.

The width of the tooth is equal to half of the circular pitch; the other half is, of course, equal to the space.

$$\text{Therefore } \frac{4.5 \text{ degrees}}{2} = 2.25 \text{ degrees,}$$

of which 2.25 degrees is the width of the tooth and 2.25 degrees the width of the space.

Next, place the generating circle B 2.25 degrees to the right of line C. With the generating circle (indicated by the dotted circle E) now centered on line D, fit a pencil marker as previously explained and roll the generating circle to the left. The pencil point will trace out the other side of the tooth as shown by dotted line D. The intersection of the two curves C and D forms the point of the tooth.

The *dedenda* of the pinion leaves is determined by the same generating circle that gave us the shape of the addenda for the wheel teeth. The method differs, however; for the generating circle is rolled inside and along the pitch circle of the pinion, producing the radial line A, as shown in Figure 7. The line formed by rolling a circle within a circle is called a *hypocycloid*.

ACTION OF CYCLOIDAL GEARING

When a wheel and pinion are made to conform with the above principles of design, constant angular velocity

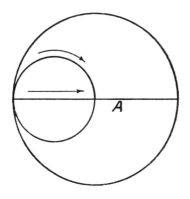

FIGURE 7
Generation of the leaf pinion.

from wheel to pinion is maintained. In studying Figure 5 it might seem that the pinion would be driven more rapidly during the latter portion of the cycle because the rotation of the gears has the effect of lengthening the wheel teeth and shortening the pinion leaves. This is not true, however, for there is a slipping action equal to half of the width of the tooth, and it is this action which equalizes their angular velocity.

The incoming tooth of the wheel should begin pressing on a pinion leaf as near as possible to the line of centers, allowing for the fact that this is a varying quantity depending on the number of leaves in the pinion. If the depthing is correct it will be found that a ten-leaf pinion begins action on the line of centers; whereas an eight-leaf pinion begins 10 degrees before the line of centers, and a six-leaf pinion begins 18 degrees before the line of centers. This is illustrated in Figure 8.

CORRECT SIZES OF WHEELS AND PINIONS

FINDING THE PITCH DIAMETER

In order to determine the correct sizes of wheels and pinions, it is first necessary to find the pitch diameters.

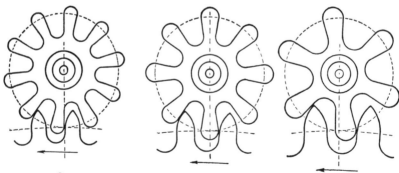

FIGURE 8
Beginning of action of ten-, eight- and six-leaf pinion respectively.

For this we proceed as follows: Adjust the male centers of the depthing tool to the two holes in a clock plate in which a wheel and pinion are to rotate. Measure the distance outside the two spindles with a vernier caliper and subtract the diameter of one spindle. This gives us the center distance for one wheel and pinion. To arrive at the pitch diameters, determine the diametrical pitch. For doing this, the formula reads as follows:

$$\frac{\text{center distance} \times 2}{\text{teeth of wheel} + \text{leaves of pinion}} = \text{diametrical pitch.}$$

The diametrical pitch is now multiplied by the number of teeth in the wheel, in order to determine the pitch diameter of the wheel, and in like manner the diametrical pitch is multiplied by the number of leaves in the pinion to determine the pitch diameter of the pinion.

For example, the center distance is 17.15 millimeters; the wheel has 42 teeth; the pinion has 7 leaves. Substituting the numerical values for the above formula, we have:

$$\frac{17.15 \times 2}{42 + 7} = .7 \text{ diametrical pitch.}$$

Continuing the problem we find that

.7 × 42 = 29.4 mm. pitch diameter of the wheel
.7 × 7 = 4.9 mm. pitch diameter of the pinion

Proof:

$$\frac{29.4 + 4.9}{2} = 17.15 \text{ mm. the distance between centers.}$$

FINDING THE FULL DIAMETER

The height of the addenda is a varying quantity, depending on the ratio of the wheel to the pinion, but the production of theoretically correct gears or even knowing when they exist is not possible with the equipment available to the practical clock repairer. The usual practice is to add 2.5 diametrical pitches to the pitch diameter of the wheel and 1.25 diametrical pitches to the pitch diameter of the pinion. There is one exception to the above statement, however. For the dial train where the pinions drive the wheels and wheels drive the pinions, as is the case when the hands are set to time, the addenda is figured as 2 for both wheels and pinions.

Returning to the main train, we found that the wheel has for its pitch diameter 29.4 millimeters and the pinion 4.9 millimeters. The diametrical pitch multiplied by 2.5 gives us the height of the addenda for the wheel teeth:

$$.7 \times 2.5 = 1.75.$$

Adding this to the pitch diameter of the wheel, we have:

$$29.4 + 1.75 = 31.15 \text{ mm. full diameter of the wheel.}$$

Now, figuring the pinion we have:

$$.7 \times 1.25 = .875.$$

Adding this to the pitch diameter of the pinion, we have:

$$4.9 + .875 = 5.775 \text{ mm. full diameter of the pinion.}$$

FINDING THE CIRCULAR PITCH

It will be noted that the definition for circular pitch reads somewhat like the definition for diametrical pitch. The difference is, however, that circular pitch is the division of the circumference of a circle (the pitch circle), whereas diametrical pitch is the division of the diameter of a circle (the pitch diameter). In both cases the number of teeth or leaves is the divisor.

We must know the actual width of tooth and space in order to select a cutter to make the wheel. Herein lies the importance of calculating the circular pitch. To do this we make use of the following formula:

$$\frac{\text{pitch diameter} \times 3.1416}{\text{teeth or leaves}} = \text{circular pitch.}$$

Substituting the numerical values:

$$\frac{29.4 \times 3.1416}{42} = 2.199 \text{ mm. circular pitch.}$$

The proportion of tooth or leaf to space is usually:

—for wheels, one-half of the circular pitch;
—for pinions, one-third of the circular pitch.

Now, continuing with the above information we find that:

$$\frac{2.199}{2} = 1.099 \text{ mm. width of the tooth, and}$$

$$\frac{2.199}{3} = .733 \text{ mm. the width of the leaf.}$$

LANTERN PINIONS

The lantern pinion gets its name from the fact that it looks like an old-fashioned lantern. The leaves are made from round steel pins and are mounted between brass disks. Lantern pinions are used in alarm clocks and in popular-priced mantel clocks. Two lantern pinions are shown in Figure 9.

The wheel that drives the lantern pinion has cycloidal teeth. The pitch circle for the pinion passes through the central part of the pins. It is a curious fact that the incoming tooth of the wheel drives the pins of the lantern pinion on the line of centers. There is no exception to this, even in

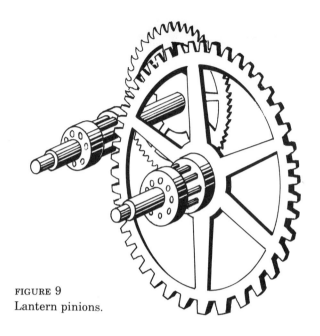

FIGURE 9
Lantern pinions.

a lantern with six pins. Suppose, however, the lantern pinion was to act as the driver. All the action would then take place before the line of centers, and the engaging friction would be very great. In fact, there is some doubt that the train would run at all. It follows, as a matter of course, that the lantern pinion is never used as a driver. As a follower it is equal, and possibly superior, to any other type of pinion in spite of the fact that it is cheaply made.

ESCAPEMENTS FOR PENDULUM CLOCKS

Probably the earliest escapement designed especially for driving the pendulum was conceived by Galileo Galilei, the great Italian astronomer, mathematician and physicist, in 1610. He made a drawing of it which has been preserved, but a working model was not made until after his death. Galileo's escapement will be described in this chapter, together with another escapement, the verge, which Christiaan Huygens, Dutch mathematician and physicist, used in his pendulum clocks. Following this, modern escapements will be described in detail.

Escapements used today may be divided into four classes. The first is the *recoil,* the oldest type that is still in use. It is found in shelf clocks, wall clocks, and antique grandfather clocks. The second is the *dead-beat* form gen-

27

erally found in regulators and the newer grandfather clocks. The third class is the *gravity* escapement. In this type the impulse is delivered to the pendulum by means of levers impelled by gravity. Gravity escapements are used almost exclusively in tower clocks. The fourth class is a precision escapement associated with what is termed *free pendulums* and its use is confined to astronomical and scientific work where great accuracy is required.

GALILEO'S ESCAPEMENT

Galileo, after observing the swinging chandelier in the Cathedral of Pisa, suggested that the pendulum could be used in clocks for controlling the time. He made a drawing of an escapement, the mechanical principle of which is shown in Figure 10. After his death in 1642 his son made a working model of the escapement. Many other models have been made. A typical one is shown in Figure 11.

The action of the escapement is shown in Figure 10. The pendulum, swinging to the left, carries with it the impulse pallet *I* and also the unlocking pallet *U*. The pallet *U* lifts the locking piece *L,* thus releasing the tooth *T*. The wheel is now free to turn and impulse pin *P* engages the impulse pallet *I,* thereby giving impulse to the pendulum, driving it to the right. Simultaneously the unlocking pallet *U* drops and permits the locking piece *L* to engage the on-coming tooth of the wheel. When the pendulum returns after completing its swing to the right, the unlocking pallet again lifts the locking piece and the action is repeated.

The chronometer escapement, although using a balance and hairspring, comprises the same mechanical principle as does this escapement by Galileo. It is a fact worth noting that the chronometer, perfected 140 years

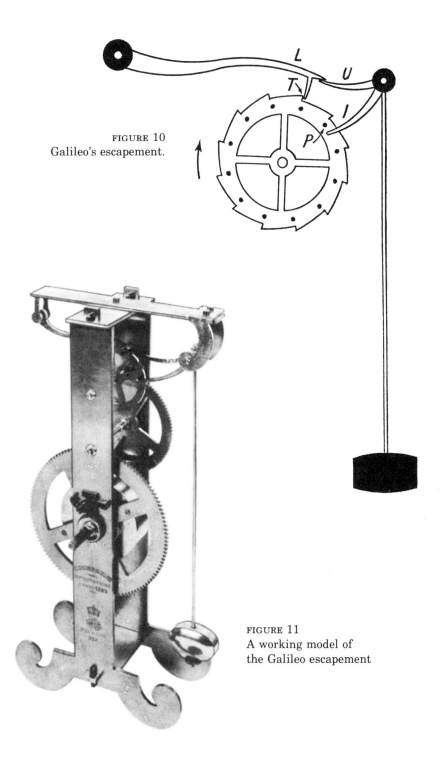

FIGURE 10
Galileo's escapement.

FIGURE 11
A working model of
the Galileo escapement

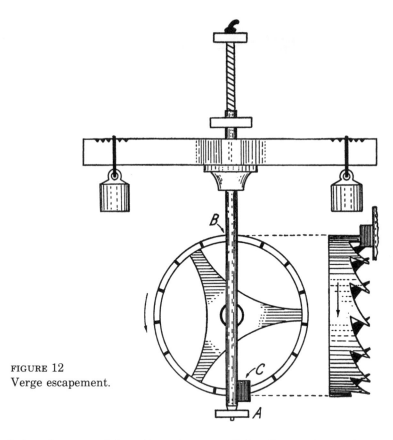

FIGURE 12
Verge escapement.

later, is a precision timepiece used for determining longitude at sea. The Galileo escapement with pendulum is not used today.

VERGE ESCAPEMENT

The first mechanical clocks—that is, those having toothed wheels and pinions and driven by a weight—date from the tenth century. The earliest escapement that attained any prominence was the *verge*. Its inventor is unknown, although the name of Pope Sylvester II (950–1003), who was learned in mathematics and astronomy, has been mentioned.

The time counter for the earliest verge clocks was a horizontal bar called the *foliot*. This can be seen in Figure 12. It is a sort of balance upon which two weights are suspended from notches near each end. The weights can be moved toward or away from the center of the foliot for the purpose of regulating the clock.

The action of the escapement is shown in Figure 12. Note that the escape wheel is shown turning in the direction of the arrow.The tooth under the pallet *B* is in the act of giving impulse. Pushing pallet *B* to the left, the tooth eventually escapes, permitting the escape wheel to turn

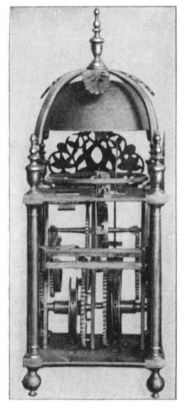

FIGURE 13
Back and front views of clock fitted with verge escapement.

until another tooth engages pallet C. After a recoil due to the inertia of the foliot, another tooth delivers impulse to pallet C, this time pushing the pallet to the right. Soon a tooth escapes and the action is repeated when another tooth engages pallet B.

It is a peculiarity of the verge escapement that the escape wheel must have an odd number of teeth in order to work. The usual number is 13 or 15 for small clocks and 21, 31, or 33 for large clocks. A clock fitted with a verge escapement is shown in Figure 13.

Huyghens adapted the pendulum to the verge escapement in about the year 1657. This was considered to be quite an achievement in his day, since the use of the pendulum had proved the definite possibility of creating a superior timepiece. Huyghens's clock using the verge escapement and pendulum is shown in Figure 14.

RECOIL ESCAPEMENT

The recoil escapement was invented by Dr. Robert Hooke in 1671. It is also sometimes referred to as the anchor escapement because its shape resembles that of an anchor. The construction is simple. The escape wheel is of brass and the number of teeth vary greatly, depending on the type of clock and the length of the pendulum. The pallets are made of steel, hardened and highly polished.

The action of the recoil escapement is shown in Figure 15. Let us start with the pendulum swinging to the left, and carrying with it the pallets. Following the impulse that reaches the pendulum, a tooth of the escape wheel drops from the receiving pallet A. The wheel is now free to turn, but its motion is immediately arrested because of contact of a tooth with the discharging pallet B. Eventually, at the completion of the impulse, the discharging pallet releases the tooth and another tooth engages the

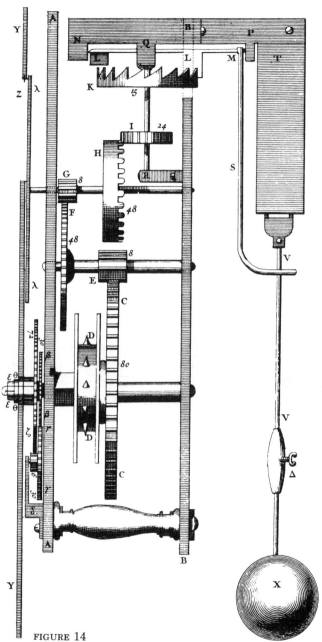

FIGURE 14
Huyghens's clock with verge escapement
and pendulum.

receiving pallet. Thus the action continues so long as the proper motive power is attained.

The recoil escapement gets its name from the fact that the escape wheel recoils, or reverses its direction, immediately after a tooth drops on a pallet. This action takes place because the pallets have no locking faces. Hence a tooth falls directly on the curved impulse face and as the pendulum continues to swing outward, the curved pallet pushes the tooth back until the pendulum completes a vibration and starts in the reverse direction. The actual impulse to the pendulum is found by subtracting the recoil from the forward motion of the escape wheel.

DEAD-BEAT ESCAPEMENT

George Graham invented the dead-beat escapement in 1715. It is still regarded as one of the best escapements

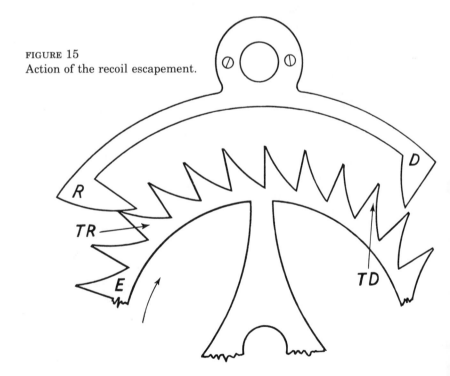

FIGURE 15
Action of the recoil escapement.

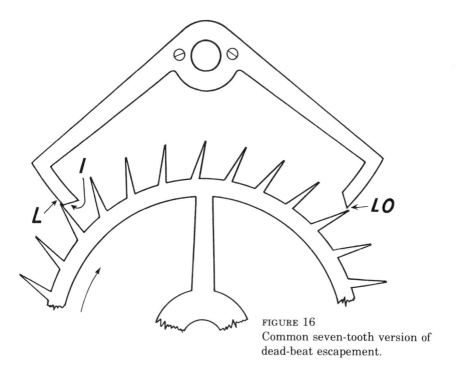

FIGURE 16
Common seven-tooth version of
dead-beat escapement.

for high-grade regulators, grandfather clocks, and other
clocks of the better quality. Except by comparison with the
finest precision clocks, this escapement leaves little to be
desired. Its only defect lies in a slight tendency to undergo
a change in the rate of running after the oil has thickened
or deteriorated.

The Graham dead-beat escapement, as seen today, is
so designed that the pallet spans seven teeth of the escape
wheel. See Figure 16. There is another design, however, in
which the pallet spans ten teeth of the escape wheel. This
version is shown in Figure 17.

The action of the dead-beat escapement is similar to
the recoil escapement described above. One point of difference, however, should be noted. When examining the action, make certain that the teeth of the escape wheel are
dropping on the locking faces and not on the impulse faces.
If not, this error could be due to worn pivot holes, because

the dead-beat escapement calls for greater precision than is required in the recoil escapement.

If the impulse of the Graham dead-beat escapement could be delivered to the pendulum an equal distance before and after the dead point, the time of swing would not be altered and there would be no escapement error. This cannot quite be realized in practice, although the Graham escapement does approach this ideal condition closely. There is about one degree of impulse before the dead point and two degrees after the dead point. The analysis on page 52 shows that an impulse delivered after the pendulum reaches the dead point results in a loss, but the Graham escapement shows a gain when the pendulum arc becomes shorter. Since it is known that the impulse area is small, the disturbing factor is more likely to be the circular error described on page 55 which, in itself, shows a gain for the short arcs.

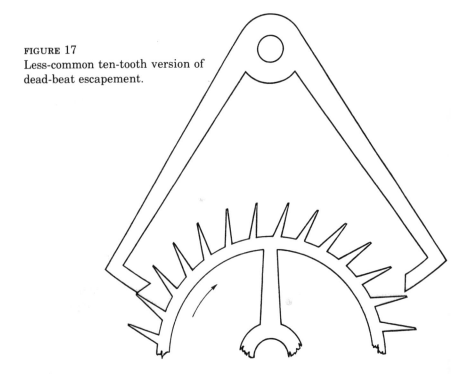

FIGURE 17
Less-common ten-tooth version of dead-beat escapement.

OBSOLETE ESCAPEMENTS

In addition to the recoil and dead-beat escapements, there are many other escapements that have been used in the past. Two of these, at one time quite popular, are the *pin-wheel,* shown in Figure 18, and the *pin-pallet,* shown in Figure 19. Both are now regarded as obsolete. In any case, their function is similar to those escapements already considered. However, there are two escapements built on entirely different principles of operation which will now be considered. These are the *gravity escapement* and the *Reifer escapement.*

DENISON'S GRAVITY ESCAPEMENT

The gravity escapement by E. B. Denison was originally designed in 1854 for Big Ben, the famous House of

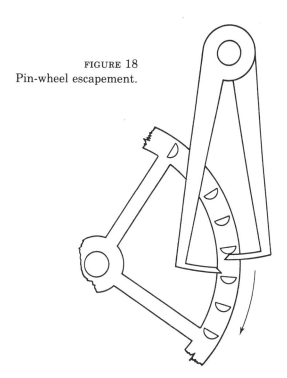

FIGURE 18
Pin-wheel escapement.

FIGURE 19
Pin-pallet escapement.

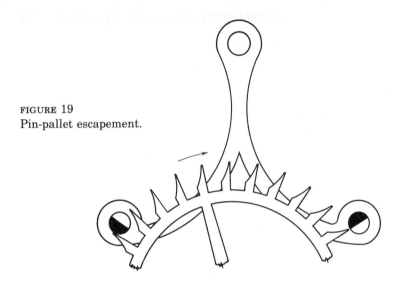

Parliament clock in London. Perhaps no other tower clock has ever earned a better reputation for accurate timekeeping. The fine performance must be ascribed to the Denison gravity escapement, for, when the escapement is thoroughly studied, two very important points become manifest:

1. The impulse to the pendulum is entirely free of such train disturbances as variations in the motive power.

2. The impulse starts at the time when the pendulum completes its outward swing and continues during the inward swing until the dead point is reached. This has a quickening effect on the pendulum and tends to compensate for the circular error.

Figure 20 shows the construction of the Denison escapement. Two gravity impulse arms A and A' are pivoted as nearly as possible to the bending point of the pendulum spring. The escape wheel W consists of two thin metal pieces of three legs each, separated by three pins, called *lifting pins*. The impulse arms A and A' lie midway between the two metal pieces. In the illustration, the light, three-legged piece stands in front of the impulse arms and the shaded piece behind the arms. Attached to the impulse arms are the blocks B and B', upon which the legs of the escape wheel lock. Block B' is secured on the front of the arm A' and block B on the back of arm A. Extending toward the lifting pins L and L' from the impulse arms are the lifting pallets P and P'.

The action of the Denison escapement is as follows: A leg of the escape wheel is locked on block B', overlapping it by ½ degree. The position of the impulse arm A' and the

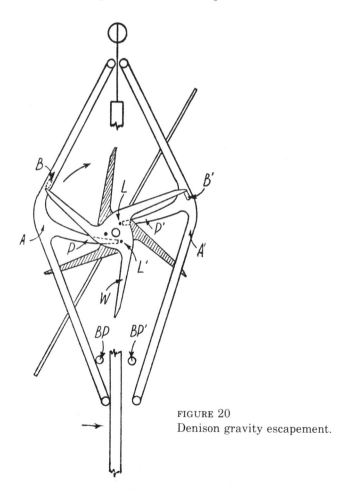

FIGURE 20
Denison gravity escapement.

amount of locking on B' is controlled by the lifting pin L acting on the lifting pallet P'.

The pendulum, now moving to the right, soon engages the lower extremity of the impulse arm A' and, pushing it, releases the leg that is locked on block B'. The escape wheel starts to rotate and the lifting pin L separates from the lifting pallet P', leaving the impulse arm A' free to press on the pendulum rod, thereby being ready to give impulse to the pendulum on its return vibration. At the same instant, while the wheel is rotating, lifting pin L' engages the lifting pallet P, pushing the impulse arm A outward so that the oncoming leg of the escape wheel locks on the block B overlapping it ½ degree. Thus the impulse arm A is pushed back in advance of the pendulum.

The pendulum, having completed its vibration to the right, receives impulse from the impulse arm A', which falls with the pendulum to the left until the banking pin BP' is reached. The pendulum continues to swing to the left for a performance similar to the one just completed on the right.

REIFER ESCAPEMENT

In the recoil and dead-beat escapements, any variation in the motive power is carried directly to the pendulum, resulting in a noticeable variation in time. The gravity escapement shows a constantly uniform impulse, but the locking is variable, depending on the power transmitted through the train.

In 1891 Dr. Siegmund Reifer of Munich produced a clock with a free pendulum—that is, an escapement without the conventional crutch. Instead of a crutch, the impulse is produced by deflecting the pendulum spring. Figure 21 shows the principle on which the escapement is based, but without all the constructional details. There

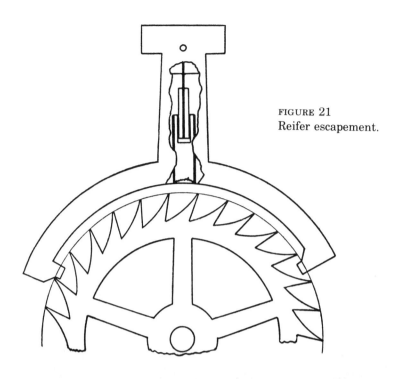

FIGURE 21
Reifer escapement.

are two escape wheels. One is for the impulse and the other for the locking. The impulse wheel acts on cylindrical pallets for the impulse and, when the impulse is completed, the locking wheel follows immediately to lock the pallets. The outer ends of the pallets are flattened to provide a suitable locking surface for the locking wheel.

The action of the escapement is as follows: The receiving pallet is locked on the locking wheel and starts the pendulum swinging to the left. After the pendulum, together with the pallets, has traveled a sufficient distance, the receiving pallet unlocks, permitting the escape wheels to rotate. Instantly the discharging pallet receives an impulse followed by a tooth locking—an order completely reversed if compared with the Graham dead-beat escapement. This action deflects the pendulum spring, which, by the resistance it offers to bending, gives impulse to the pendulum. Observe that this happens before the pendulum has as yet completed its swing to the left. The outward swing of the pendulum is thus restricted and, when the arc is completed, the tension on the pendulum spring is sufficient to keep the pendulum swinging.

It may be reasoned that the good going of the Reifer clock is attributable to the small arc of swing of the pendulum and the uniform motive power which consists of an automatic electrical winding device.

 **4** **PENDULUMS**

For three hundred years the pendulum has been a most important piece of clockwork. It is practically a precision instrument for the measurement of time. By means of a weight or mainspring, a train of wheels and an escapement, its swinging motion—which friction and the resistance of the air tend to destroy—can be sustained indefinitely. In order to discuss the theory of the pendulum with any degree of clearness, it is necessary to digress for a moment and consider some of the factors concerning the earth upon which we live. The rotation of the earth on its axis, the nature of gravitation, and many other physical phenomena all have a direct bearing on the observed performance of the pendulum.

TABLE 1
HOW FALL OF BODY INCREASES WITH DISTANCE COVERED

Duration of fall	Distance covered	Velocity per second
1 sec.	16 ft.	32 ft./sec. after 1 sec.
2 "	64 "	64 " " " 2 "
3 "	144 "	96 " " " 3 "
4 "	256 "	128 " " " 4 "
5 "	400 "	256 " " " 5 "

UNIVERSAL FORCES

GRAVITATION

All bodies fall perpendicularly with reference to the surface of still water. In other words, they fall vertically, which is, of course, toward the center of the earth. The fall of a body also increases in velocity through the distance covered as shown in Table 1.

The above table shows that in two seconds a body falls four times as far as it falls in the first second. In three seconds a body falls nine times as far; in four seconds, sixteen times as far. Thus, we may say that the distance which a body falls is proportional to the square of time.

NEWTON'S LAW OF UNIVERSAL GRAVITATION*

Sir Isaac Newton (1642–1727) discovered certain facts about gravity, known ever since as Newton's Law:

---

*Newton's system of mechanics as explained above is valid for the pendulum and other large-scale phenomena of nature. However, the theory of relativity has shown that beyond these lies a system of atomic and subatomic processes which do not obey Newton's laws at all. See H. Horton Sheldon, *Space, Time and Relativity,* The University Society, New York.

All bodies in the universe attract every other body with a force which is directly proportional to the product of the attracting masses and inversely proportional to the square of the distances between their centers.

This statement of the law may be clarified by elaborating on it as follows:

Gravity acts between bodies, and the attraction is proportional to the mass—that is, a larger mass carries with it an equally increased pull of gravity. This was demonstrated by Galileo, when he was professor of physics at the University of Pisa. He dropped large and small iron balls from the leaning tower of Pisa. They reached the ground at the same time. This demonstration astonished and bewildered a number of professors who saw it, for prior to that time it had been believed that heavy bodies fell faster than light bodies.

Later, after the invention of the air pump for producing a vacuum, this statement by Galileo was verified by demonstrating that heavy and light bodies such as a coin and a feather would fall together in a glass tube where they did not encounter the friction of the air. After the air was again admitted, the feather would flutter slowly behind the rapidly falling coin.

Newton further proved that gravity is the same as though the entire mass of the body was concentrated at its center. Hence, in considering the attraction of the earth for any body on its surface, the distance indicated in the law is the earth's radius plus the distance to the center of gravity of the body.

Newton's law goes on to state that the attraction of the masses is inversely proportional to the square of the distance between their centers. For example, let us suppose that a body was removed twice as far from the earth's center and allowed to fall. It would fall only one-fourth as fast. If removed three, four, or five times as far from the earth's center, the body would fall one-ninth, one-sixteenth, or one twenty-fifth as fast. Hence, an iron ball would fall faster when dropped at an altitude of sea level than an iron ball dropped on a mountain 7,000 feet above sea level. This fact can be proved when counting the vibrations of a pendulum placed at different altitudes.

CENTRIFUGAL FORCE

Tie a string to a stone and whirl it rapidly around your head. The string will stretch tighter and tighter. Increase the speed and there is a possibility that the string will break. If so, the stone will fly away at a tangent. This thrust is known as *centrifugal force* and tends to distort a sphere rotating on its axis. In fact, this earth of ours bulges at the equator and is flattened at the poles due to this very same cause, for the earth is sufficiently pliable to be so formed. As a result of this bulging of the land and water about the equator, the earth is 26.7 miles shorter between the poles than through the equator.

Centrifugal force is greatest at the equator and decreases with each parallel of latitude toward the poles. At the poles it is zero and the weight of all bodies is affected accordingly.

DEFINITIONS

Now, returning to the study of the pendulum, we shall see how the earth's motion and gravitation affect the performance of the pendulum. It is desirable, however, to consider, first, several definitions relative to the subject.

PENDULUM: Any suspended body that swings to and fro.
BOB: The mass of metal at the bottom of the pendulum.

SIMPLE PENDULUM: A heavy bob suspended by a slender thread.

COMPOUND PENDULUM: Any pendulum having a portion of its mass elsewhere than in a compact bob. All clock pendulums are compound pendulums.

CENTER OF SUSPENSION: The fixed support of a pendulum.

CENTER OF OSCILLATION: A point in the bob in which if all the matter composing the bob were collected into it the time of swinging would not be affected.

VIBRATION: One complete swing of the pendulum.

PERIOD: Time occupied in making one vibration.

AMPLITUDE: The angle between the vertical and the end of a vibration. In Figure 22 Angle AOB is the amplitude.

MOTION OF THE PENDULUM

We know that the simple pendulum is in equilibrium when the thread which supports the bob is vertical. How-

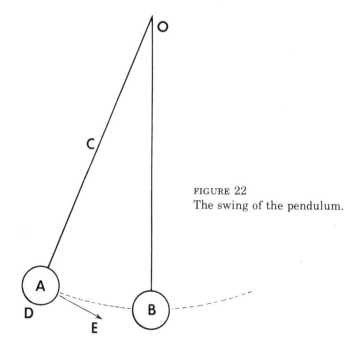

FIGURE 22
The swing of the pendulum.

ever, if we pull the pendulum bob to an inclined position and let it go, it will descend to regain its original position and its own momentum will cause it to rise nearly as far on the opposite side.

The gravity that acts on the bob when it is in motion is a vertical force which may be separated into two parts: The first part acts with the prolongation of the thread as at D, in Figure 22. This force does not show because of the thread C which supports the bob. The second acts in a direction perpendicular to the first, as at E, and manifests all its force through the vertical attraction of gravity on the bob, thus forcing the bob along the line AB. The bob will move along a circular path with an accelerated movement but not consistently so, as with a falling body, for the gravitational force along the circular path is continually diminishing and ceases altogether when the bob reaches the vertical position. On regaining its vertical position the pendulum will rise on the opposite side because of its acquired momentum, although gravity will now act as a retarding force and the velocity will be lessened. It will, however, rise to nearly the same height that it left on the other side and then return, executing another swing like the first.

It is an interesting fact that a simple pendulum would vibrate for all time if friction and resistance of the air could be completely eliminated, but obviously this cannot be done.

When a pendulum is taken from one location to another in which the force of gravity is different, its rate is affected in the same manner as that of a falling body and for the same reason. Thus it follows that a pendulum clock regulated to keep time at the equator would run fast at the poles. In fact the length of a seconds pendulum for points on the earth's surface (at sea level) would be as shown on the facing page.

TABLE 2
LENGTH OF PENDULUM

Location	Length (inches)
Equator	39
Rio de Janeiro	39.01
New York	39.10
Paris	39.13
The poles	39.206

THE PENDULUM FORMULA

The laws governing the action of the pendulum are expressed in the following formula:

$$t = \pi \sqrt{\frac{l}{g}}$$

in which t = the time of one vibration (period)
π = 3.1416 which is the relation of the circumference to the diameter
l = the length of the pendulum
g = the acceleration of gravity

By means of this formula we may determine: (1) the length of a pendulum for a given period; (2) the period for a given length of the pendulum; and (3) the acceleration of gravity for any point on the earth's surface. Clock repairers are, of course, interested only in the first two principles and therefore the third will not be considered further.

EXAMPLE 1. What is the length of a seconds pendulum if the acceleration of gravity is 32.2 feet (386.4 inches) per second?

$$t = \pi \sqrt{\frac{l}{g}}$$

$$1 = 3.14 \sqrt{\frac{l}{386.4}}$$

$$1^2 = \frac{9.8696l}{386.4}$$

$$\frac{9.8696l}{386.4} = 1^2 \text{ or } 1$$

$$l = \frac{1 \times 386.4}{9.8696}$$

$$l = 39.1505$$

EXAMPLE 2. What is the period of a pendulum 9.75 inches long?

$$t = 3.1416 \sqrt{\frac{9.75}{386.4}}$$

$$t^2 = \frac{9.8696 \times 9.75}{386.4}$$

$$t^2 = .2491, \text{ or } .25$$

$$t = .5 \text{ or } \tfrac{1}{2} \text{ second}$$

The solution of the above problems may be simplified by noting that the pendulum formula includes the following:

$$t = \sqrt{l}$$

Squaring we have

$$t^2 = l$$

Thus we may consider two of different periods and their relative lengths by the proportion:

$$t^2 : l :: t_2^2 : l_2$$

It follows that the length or period of any pendulum can be determined if the length of a second pendulum is known.

EXAMPLE 3. What is the length of a pendulum vibrating ⅓ seconds?

$$1^2 : 39 :: (⅓)^2 : l$$

$$1/39 = \frac{(⅓)^2}{l}$$

$$l = 1/9 \times 39$$

$$l = 4⅓ \text{ inches}$$

EXAMPLE 4. What is the period of a pendulum 156 inches long?

$$1^2 : 39 :: t^2 : 156$$

$$1/39 = \frac{t^2}{156}$$

$$\frac{156}{39} = t^2$$

$$t^2 = \frac{156}{39} = 4$$

$$t = 2 \text{ seconds}$$

DETRIMENTAL FORCES

There are several forces that alter the uniform swing of the pendulum. Some can be accurately controlled, but others cannot. The more important errors are as follows:

Escapement error
Barometric error
Circular error
Temperature error

ESCAPEMENT ERROR

The impulse delivered to the pendulum through the escapement should take place at the moment when the pendulum reaches the dead point—that is, when the pendulum is vertical. This ideal condition would permit the pendulum to swing to and fro in the same time that a free pendulum performs these swings. However, the mechanical means at our disposal to keep the pendulum swinging do not meet the above requirements and we are obliged to take account of the following laws:

An impulse delivered to the pendulum before the dead point will accelerate the vibrations.

An impulse delivered to the pendulum after the dead point will retard the vibrations.

This can be easily demonstrated with a simple pendulum. Impulse given to a pendulum before it reaches the dead point causes it to arrive at the dead point more quickly than if it were acted upon by gravity alone. An impulse delivered after the pendulum has reached the dead point simply drives the pendulum farther, resisting the force of gravity, but at no particularly accelerated rate, if any. Hence the overall result is that a retardation takes place, and the greater the distance the impulse takes place after the dead point, the greater is the retardation.

BAROMETRIC ERROR

A swinging pendulum fans the air and creates a breeze in its wake much like that of a rapidly moving train. Much more happens than the mere disturbance of the air, and to clarify the subject it will be necessary first to explain some of the phenomena relative to the atmosphere.

Air, like all gases, is made up of untold millions of molecules. These molecules move about freely and at a terrific speed. Their constant motion produces a pressure of great magnitude and the higher the temperature the faster is the motion and the greater is the pressure. Atmospheric pressure is fifteen pounds to a square inch, or about one ton to a square foot. This pressure takes place in every direction. Since air is a real substance occupying space, it must have weight. Experiments have shown that a cubic foot of air weighs 1¼ ounces and that the air in an average living room weighs about 500 pounds.

The above analysis of the atmosphere leaves no doubt that the swing of the pendulum would be affected. If the weight and pressure of the air were constant, these factors would be of little concern to clockmakers, but since they are variable, the pendulum arcs vary also. Atmosphere affects the pendulum by way of three forces. These are: *(1) inertia of the air; (2) friction of the air; and (3) weight of the pendulum.*

(1) Inertia of the air. When a pendulum starts on its downward swing, it must, of necessity, push the air, but as the inertia of the air is overcome, the air travels along with the pendulum. If the resistance of the air before and after the dead point were equal, the time of the swing would not be altered. It can be shown, however, that the resistance of the air is greater as the pendulum approaches the dead point and less after it passes the dead point. This is clear when one realizes that the downward swing of the pendulum is constantly being accelerated and consequently has to push the air all the way to the dead point. In its upward swing, the pendulum is retarded by gravity and from that point on the air just about keeps up with the pendulum. Thus the inertia of the air tends to prolong the time of the downward swing and also extends the time of

the upward swing. The total result is a loss in time, and with a rising temperature (high barometer) and its associated increase in air pressure, the loss becomes still greater.

(2) *Friction of the air.* The friction of the air on the pendulum leads us to a discussion of the best shape for the bob. Tower and precision clocks usually use the cylindrical bob. Most others use the lens-shaped bob. The cylindrical bob is subject to more air resistance than the lens-shaped bob, yet the latter meets with more surface friction. The more detrimental force is the air resistance, particularly if the pendulum is enclosed in a case. It is a simple matter to demonstrate this by making two bobs of equal mass and material, one cylindrical and one lens-shaped. By causing them to vibrate without an escapement, we may observe with which kind of bob the arc of vibration falls off more quickly. The lens-shaped bob swings longer, which also implies that it would take less power through the escapement to keep it swinging. Against this slight advantage, the clock designer must take into account the fact that the temperature factor can be more easily controlled in the cylindrical bob. It is for this reason that the cylindrical bob is frequently used in precision clocks. For example, many regulators use the Graham mercury pendulum, which is cylindrical.

(3) *Weight of the pendulum.* We have just learned that air, like all substances, has weight, and because of this, all masses heavier than air tend to be buoyed up. Every swimmer has observed that it takes less effort to lift a heavy stone at the bottom of a swimming pool than to lift the same stone above ground. The effect is similar with the pendulum in air; for, with a denser atmosphere, the apparent weight or pull of gravity on the bob is reduced and

the clock tends to run slower. This loss of gravitational pull due to buoyancy varies with the specific gravity of the metal used for the bob. It is greatest with iron and least with lead. Brass lies midway between. The solution to the barometric problem in precision clocks is to partially remove the air from the pendulum chamber and maintain a constant temperature. For domestic clocks the error is too small to be of any concern.

CIRCULAR ERROR

Christiaan Huyghens, who built the first pendulum clock in 1657, identified a problem that clockmakers to this day have not solved. He observed that the pendulum is not isochronous, and that as a result the long arcs lose and the short arcs gain. Also, the change of rate is not uniform to the change of arc. Instead, the loss increases more rapidly as the arcs become consistently longer. Huyghens called this error the *circular error*. The change of rate for different amplitudes is shown in Table 3.

TABLE 3
CHANGE OF RATE FOR DIFFERENT AMPLITUDES

Semi-arc	Seconds per day
30′	.41
1° 00′	1.65
1° 30′	3.7
2° 00′	6.6
2° 30′	10.3
3° 00′	14.8

The circular error was a real problem in Huyghens's clock, for the verge escapement of his day vibrated with an exceedingly long arc. Huyghens developed a theoretical

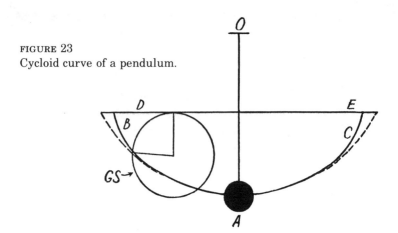

FIGURE 23
Cycloid curve of a pendulum.

solution, but it has never been given a practical application. Theoretically the problem is simple, for all the pendulum bob has to do is to follow the path of a cycloid as shown in Figure 23. The dotted line shows the path of the pendulum bob. The solid line *BC* shows the path of the cycloid. To make the cycloidal curve, fit a pencil marker to a point on the circumference of the circle *GS* (the generating circle), and roll it along the line *DE,* without slipping. The curve *BC* is thus formed. The diameter of the generating circle is half the length of the pendulum *OA*. It is at once evident that the steeper sides of the cycloidal path would give the pendulum added impulse that would make the long and short pendulum swings isochronous.

As a practical solution, Huyghens conceived the idea of using cycloidal cheeks as shown in Figure 24. The pendulum rod was suspended by two small cords and when these contacted the cheeks, the pendulum bob was forced to follow the path of a cycloid. Huyghens's pendulum has never been used with modern escapements, however, because of mechanical difficulties involved. Also, modern clocks use a different type of escapement which does not demand such a long pendulum arc, and this, alone, reduces the circular error. As a result of these refinements and changes, the circular error is not a problem in modern timepieces.

TEMPERATURE ERROR

Most materials of which pendulums are made expand in heat and contract in cold. Therefore a clock without some sort of temperature compensation will run *fast* in winter and *slow* in summer. The theory of compensated pendulums is simply that the center of gravity of the bob is raised or lowered to an amount equal to the lengthening or shortening of the pendulum rod. This is realized by placing the regulating nut at the bottom of the bob.

Suppose, for example, a pendulum rod of wood lowers the regulating nut a given amount with a rise in temperature. The bob is of lead and since lead expands eight times as much as wood, the diameter of the bob is one-fourth the length of the pendulum rod. The result is a fixed distance

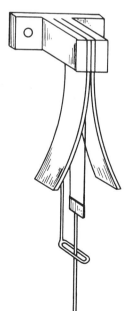

FIGURE 24
Huyghens's remedy for circular error.

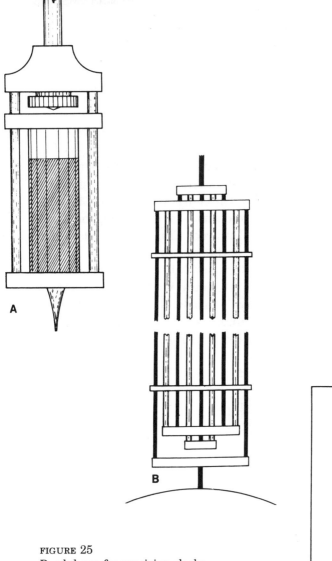
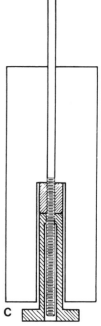

Pendulums for precision clocks.
A. Graham's mercury pendulum.
B. Harrison's gridiron pendulum.
C. Invar pendulum.

from the center of gravity of the bob to the point of suspension for all temperatures.

Wood and lead pendulums are suitable for popular-priced regulators, grandfather clocks, and domestic clocks, but are not considered sufficiently accurate for precision clocks.

Regulators of the highest quality use pendulums that register one second for each swing. These are shown in Figure 25. The theory of operation is the same as that described for the wood and lead pendulums and therefore additional comment is not needed here.

STRIKING MECHANISMS

The striking mechanism of a clock consists of a separate train and power unit. It is not in any way connected with the timekeeping mechanism, except that the main train sets the striking train in motion at the proper time. There are two types of striking mechanisms in general use. These are the counting-wheel and the rack-and-snail. The counting-wheel is the older; in fact, it is as old as the mechanical clock itself. It is still used in American shelf clocks and in tower clocks. The rack-and-snail type was invented by Edward Barlow in 1676 and is found in shelf clocks of the better quality and in all modern grandfather clocks.

The best way for a beginner to learn the fundamentals of a striking mechanism is to have a real clock movement placed in front of him. To be sure, an analysis of a drawing will give the beginner an opportunity to learn the names of the parts and their respective functions, but this is not enough. He will still need to see an actual clock movement in which he can view all the clock movement parts in their proper relationship one to the other. The beginner must see the parts in motion. By fitting the hands to the movement and pushing the minute hand slowly, the period of warning and striking may be quickly observed. It is not enough to observe the movement of the parts for one hour. This should be done for several hours and each observation should be carefully studied.

There are many different mechanical principles embodied in the clocks the clock repairer will encounter over a period of time. Each of them should be carefully studied. However, we shall now analyze two of the most common clock striking mechanisms.

COUNTING-WHEEL MECHANISM

In Figure 26 as the cam on the center arbor CA advances clockwise and raises the lifting lever L, four levers are brought into action. Warning lever W is raised into position to engage the pin P on the warning wheel. The unlocking lever U lifts the drop lever D and also the counting lever CL, since both levers are attached to the arbor B. This results in a simultaneous separation of these two levers from their seats—the former from the notch in the cam wheel and the latter from the deeper slot in the counting-wheel. The train is now free to turn, but only for a moment, because pin P on the warning wheel will catch on the already raised warning lever W. Precisely on the hour, the cam on the center arbor CA passes the lifting lever L, permitting the lifting lever to fall. At the same moment, the warning lever W also drops. This action re-

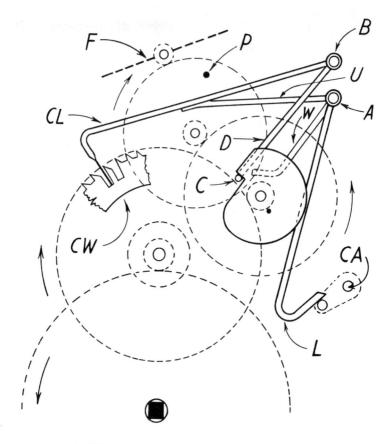

FIGURE 26
Counting-wheel mechanism.

leases the pin P on the warning wheel and the striking begins. The speed of the striking mechanism is controlled by the Fly F. As the striking continues, the counting-wheel turns, and the counting lever drops into and rises above the shallow slots. Finally, the counting lever drops into one of the deeper slots, and the drop lever, at the same moment, drops into the notch on the cam wheel. When this happens, the striking stops.

RACK-AND-SNAIL MECHANISM

In Fig. 27 the pin *P* on the minute wheel advances in the direction of the arrow and raises the lifting piece *LP*. Then the warning lever *WL* lifts the rack hook *RH*, freeing the rack which falls to the appropriate step on the snail. At the same time the stop pin *SP* (which is attached to the rack) recedes from the tail *T* of the gathering pallet *G*, thus permitting the train to start. The train is soon stopped, however, because the pin *WP* on the warning

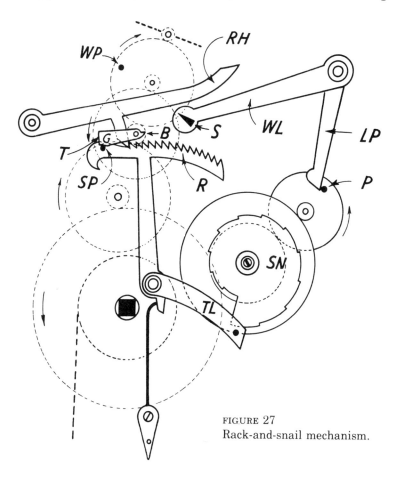

FIGURE 27
Rack-and-snail mechanism.

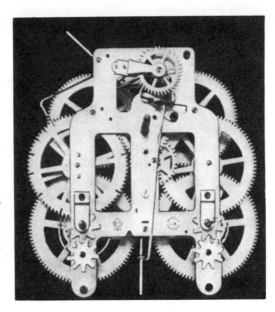

FIGURE 28
Counting-wheel
striking mechanism
from American
shelf clock.

wheel engages the stop piece *S* located on the back of the warning lever *WL*.

Later, on the hour, the pin *P* on the minute wheel passes the end of the lifting piece *LP,* permitting the warning lever *WL* to drop and free the warning wheel. The striking train is now set in motion and the beak *B* on the gathering pallet *G* proceeds to collect the teeth on the rack. After the last tooth is collected, the stop pin *SP* advances in the path of the gathering pallet's tail *T* and the striking train stops.

ERRORS IN THE WARNING SYSTEM

It often happens that after the clock has been cleaned, repaired and assembled, a timing error will show. Consider first the counting-wheel design.

Counting-wheel system. Failure of the system to stop striking at the proper time is usually due to incorrect timing.

Turn the minute hand to the hour and allow the striking to run slowly. When the counting lever drops into a deep notch in the counting-wheel, the drop lever should lock in the cam wheel. If the cam wheel is not in the proper position, the drop lever cannot lock in the notch. Let the mainsprings down or insert a watch screwdriver through the second wheel and plates to lock the train. Then separate the plates on the striking side. Separate the cam wheel from the wheels next to it and turn the cam wheel so that its notch takes a position to accept the drop lever. This is largely a trial-and-error process and several attempts may be required. Eventually the proper location will be found.

Rack-and-snail system. A faulty adjustment occasionally met with in the rack-and-snail system is incorrect timing for the striking hammer when the clock warns. This results in a lot of useless run after the striking is completed. There should be very little run after the striking and no lifting of the striking hammer during the warning.

Correction of this error consists in separating the wheels as noted above and changing the position of the wheel T (see Figure 29) so that it relates to the pinion on the warning wheel W at a different angle. This may require a changed position of the gathering pallet G. This is a simple matter, for the gathering pallet is pushed on friction tight and pliers may be used to remove the pallet. When the pallet is replaced, it must be so positioned as to clear the rack-teeth when the striking stops.

CHIMES AND CHIMING MECHANISMS

In clockmaking, sets of bells struck by hammers in order to play fascinating tunes have been popular for centuries. These bell combinations are commonly called *chimes,* and they play at quarter-hour periods. Some play one chime, whereas others play two or three. In the latter cases, the desired chime is selected by setting a hand on the clock dial. The most popular chimes are the Westminster and the Wittington.

Chiming clocks use three trains: (1) hour striking train, (2) time train, and (3) chiming train. The time train occupies the center of the movement, the hour-striking train is planted to the left, and the chiming train to the right. The rack-and-snail system is the one usually used. Occasionally one finds the counting-wheel used on the chiming train and the rack-and-snail on the hour-striking train. The mechanical principles vary somewhat in the different makes, but the most popular designs follow the plan shown in Figure 30.

FIGURE 29
Clock movement with
rack-and-snail striking.

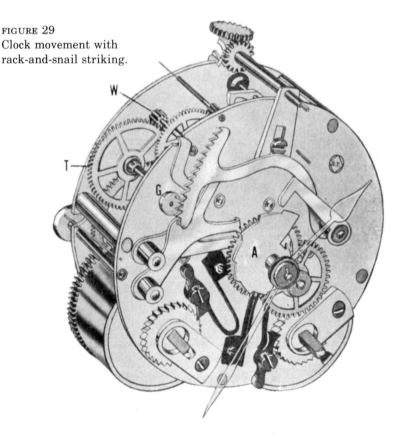

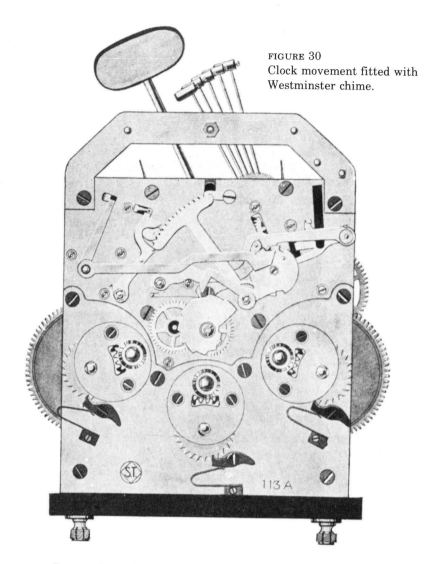

FIGURE 30
Clock movement fitted with
Westminster chime.

Correcting the timing error in the chiming train
when the clock warns does not differ from that described
above and need not be repeated here. However, it is desirable to thoroughly study all chime movements that are
received for cleaning before they are disassembled, in
order to make certain that their action is completely un-
derstood.

REPAIR
AND
RESTORATION

Dirt and the lack of lubrication will, in time, cause damage to the pivots of clock wheels. This will most commonly involve the destruction of the polished surface, although in cases of greater damage grooves or ridges may be found as well.

PIVOT REPAIRS

If the pivot is only slightly damaged, it can be restored to its original condition by fitting the wheel in a lathe and filing the pivot with a pivot file. After the rough surface has been made smooth, the pivot is finished with a steel burnisher. In many cases a new bushing will be needed to provide a smaller hole for the smaller pivot. So, it follows that our next project is the fitting of bushings.

MAKING AND FITTING BUSHINGS

The fitting of bushings is a standard procedure in clock work. Bushings of a kind that are completely ready for fitting may be purchased from tool and material dealers. In enlarging the hole to receive the bushing, it is necessary to draw back the hole to its original position, since the wear is on one side. To do this, use a needle file to center the hole. Then complete the job with a large broach. Broach out the hole from the inside of the plate and make the hole just large enough to receive the bushing. Then drive the bushing into the plate and see to it that the bushing lies flush with the plate. Then, if needed, broach out the hole to fit the pivot. Fit the wheel between the plates so as to determine the proper freedom and the necessary end shake.

On the other hand, some clock repairers prefer to make their own bushings. Bushing wire with a hole already drilled in it may be purchased from tool and material dealers. The procedure is as follows:

Secure the wire in a split chuck (an attachment of the lathe), then place the unit in the lathe and turn it to a size that will fit tightly in the hole in the plate, which has been prepared as noted above. Now polish the graver with a 4/0 emery paper and bright-cut the end of the brass wire. Turn an oil cup to the hole already drilled in the wire. Now cut off the bushing, taking note of the length required, to match the thickness of the plate. Drive the finished bushing into the plate and broach out the hole to fit the pivot of the wheel that works with it.

PIVOTING

Success in pivoting depends on the quality of the drills and in keeping the drills sharp. It is better to drill the arbor without tempering, yet there are times when tempering must be resorted to, and in such cases a small copper wire as shown in Figure 31 may be used. The leaves of the pinion are held in a pin vise or parallel pliers to prevent the heat from spreading to that part while the copper wire is heated over an alcohol lamp. The end of the arbor is tempered to a blue color.

The wheel may be centered in a split chuck. Face off the pivot to a square shoulder and turn a small center. Place a pivot drill in a pin vise and drill a hole, which should be a little deeper than the length of the average pivot. Should the drill cease to cut, sharpen it immediately. A dull drill is apt to burnish the bottom of the hole, presenting a serious problem. Should this happen, flatten the end of the drill, which usually results in the drill

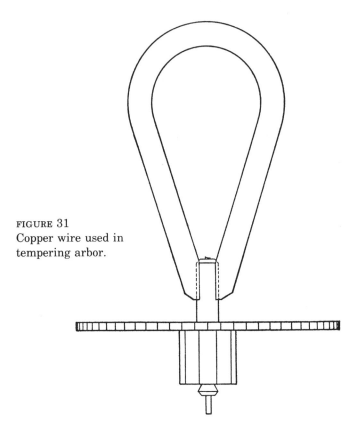

FIGURE 31
Copper wire used in
tempering arbor.

FIGURE 32
Finished pivot.

cutting again. The hole having been drilled to a satisfactory depth, secure a piece of pivot wire in a pin vise and file sufficiently to just start and hang in the hole in the arbor. Caution should be exercised in filing the wire so as to show a slight taper. Next, force the wire into the hole, cut off the wire with the cutting pliers, and tap the wire with a small hammer, thereby forcing the wire securely in the hole. The pivot is brought to size with a pivot file and polished with the burnisher. The finished pivot is shown in Figure 32.

ESCAPEMENT REPAIRS

The escape wheel is often worn at the ends of the teeth, and deep grooves may be found on the impulse faces of the pallets. If the tips of the teeth on the escape wheel are worn, they may be restored to good condition by grinding them down. Center the escape-wheel arbor in the split chuck (make certain the wheel runs in a perfect circle; no wobble) and while the lathe is running at a high speed, lightly grind the tips of the teeth with an Arkansas slip. Smooth further with a steel burnisher. This treatment reduces the diameter of the escape wheel slightly and may require an adjustment of the pallets to fit the escape wheel. An excess of inside drop may result. The correction consists in closing the pallets. The pallets must be tempered blue and then closed in a vise. Make the corrections gradually, testing the pallets to the escape wheel frequently, until the drops, both outside and inside, are found to be equal. Having found the correction satisfactory, heat the pallets to a cherry red color and plunge into water to restore the original hardness.

If the pallets have a badly worn area along the middle

of the lift, try adjusting the escape wheel or the pallet frame to a new position wherein the escape-wheel teeth will slide on a portion of the pallets that is not worn. If the pallet frame cannot be shifted, restore the pallets by first using the Arkansas slip. Slide the slip lengthwise until the groove is removed. Follow with a similar treatment using a No. 3 emery buff stick and finish the job with a steel burnisher.

CLEANING THE CLOCK MOVEMENT

Cleaning and rinsing solutions can be purchased from tool and material dealers. There are several brands on the market, and all of these are the kinds used in the ultrasonic watch-cleaning machine. Clock parts are too large to use in most ultrasonic cleaning machines. However, these ultrasonic solutions can be used successfully by pouring the solution into any metal container of sufficient size to receive the clock parts.

In addition to a container and special ultrasonic solutions, we need suitable cleaning brushes, a supply of pegwood, and two kinds of clock oil. One oil is used for the escapement, train wheels and general oiling. The second is for the mainspring. We will also need oil cups and an assortment of clock oilers.

There are many different types of clocks. The cleaning analysis that follows is designed to cover all clocks. However, special consideration has to be given to two types. One is the movement with the open mainspring, and the other is the movement with the mainspring enclosed in a barrel.

OPEN MAINSPRING

Having on hand the above cleaning items, we are now ready to clean the clock with open mainspring (Figure 34).

FIGURE 33
Double-end bench key for letting down
and winding the mainspring.

First the mainspring must be let down. This is done with
the bench key shown in Figure 33. Before doing so, however, place a spring clamp over the mainspring (Figure 34).
New mainsprings are enclosed in these clamps, and several sizes may be acquired with the purchase of mainsprings.
These should be saved for future use. An adjustable hose
clamp, such as is used on an automobile radiator hose, may
sometimes be used instead. Using the bench key that fits
the square of the winding arbor, release the click and allow
the mainspring to run down slowly by letting the wooden
handle slip between the the thumb and fingers.

Fill the container with the ultrasonic cleaning solution and drop all wheels, plates, and the larger parts into
the solution. Allow the pieces to remain in the cleaner for
about five minutes. Tip the container so as to splash the
solution in, around, and through the movement parts.
After the required soaking of all parts, lift out the parts
piece by piece and use a cleaning brush to scrub the wheels
and plates and other parts thoroughly. Frequent dipping
of the brush in the ultrasonic cleaner is advised.

The pivot holes in the plates are cleaned with pegwood. Sharpen a piece of pegwood to a point with a single-
edge razor blade. Insert the pointed end into the pivot hole
and rotate the pegwood until the hole is cleaned. Now wipe
the parts dry with a clean rag.

Fill another container with the rinsing solution.
Place the parts in the rinse and, after five minutes of
soaking, remove the parts and dry them under a heating
lamp.

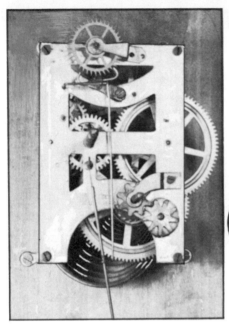

FIGURE 34
Clock movement with
open mainspring.

Assembling the movement. After the parts are dry, the movement is ready for assembly. Fit the mainspring in its place and follow with the train wheels and the escape wheel. Next, put the top plate in place and lead the wheels to their respective holes in the top plate. Now secure the top plate to the posts and fasten in place with the pins or nuts, as the case may be.

Oil the mainspring with the special mainspring oil. Then, using the regular clock oil, oil all wheel pivots and every other tooth of the escape wheel. Now fit the pallet fork complete with crutch. That part of the pendulum rod touching the slot in the crutch should receive a small spot of oil. The arbor for the pallet frame should also be oiled.

Set the movement on a shelf for a test run. Later, fit the movement into the case, adjust the beat, and complete the regulation to time.

MAINSPRING ENCLOSED IN BARREL

The dismantling, cleaning and final assembly of the clock with a barrel for the mainspring differs slightly from the clock with the open mainspring.

Using the bench key that fits the square on the barrel arbor, let the mainspring down in the manner already described. It is not necessary to use a mainspring holder in this case, since the barrel itself serves as holder. Remove the dial train. In most movements of this type, it lies on the long post of the center wheel. Remove the ratchet wheel and, in some designs, the click can be removed. Now separate the plates, remove the train wheels and proceed with the cleaning as already described, except for the barrel and its mainspring.

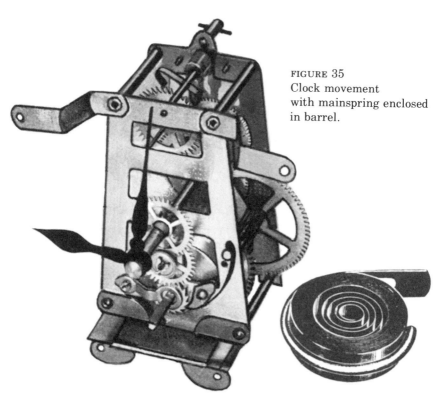

FIGURE 35
Clock movement
with mainspring enclosed
in barrel.

The cover of the mainspring barrel has a crescent-shaped slot. By inserting the blade of a small screwdriver the cover can be easily removed. Grasp the barrel arbor with pliers and turn it backwards until it unlocks from the hole in the mainspring. Then lift out the barrel arbor. If the mainspring appears clean and adequately lubricated, it is preferable to leave things as they are.

If the barrel is dirty inside and outside, then the mainspring must be removed. Secure the barrel in a vise supported by two pieces of wood. Then, with brass-faced pliers, pull out two or three coils. Lay the pliers aside and continue easing the mainspring out with the thumb and fingers. In this case the mainspring will most likely need cleaning. Dip a linen rag in the cleaning solution and draw the spring through the rag until clean. Then wipe the spring dry with a clean, dry rag.

After the barrel and mainspring have been cleaned, the mainspring is again fitted into the barrel. First see to it that the hooking of the outer end of the spring has taken effect, and that it is secured to the barrel wall. Continue with the thumb and fingers the winding in of the mainspring. This procedure is followed by oiling the mainspring and replacing the cap.

Now the movement is assembled in the manner already described. The mainspring is wound fully and the other details relative to checking the beat, running and regulating, follow in order.

PENDULUM SUSPENSION SPRINGS

Now that the clock is running, one point may have been overlooked. This has to do with the *suspension spring*. A great variety of these are shown in the Appendix.

The suspension spring should have no buckle or kink

in it. Faulty conditions of this kind in the spring will cause the pendulum to wobble. Since tool and material dealers carry a large line of suspension springs, one should not hesitate to order a new suspension spring if needed.

CLOCK REPAIRING WITHOUT A LATHE

It is apparent from my observations that I see fewer lathes on watch and clock repairers' benches. One reason for this may be the high cost of a lathe and lathe attachments. Again, there may be other reasons. One reason may be that the kind of work the repairman is called upon to do has shown considerable change. This could mean that in the general run of work, there is less need for the lathe.

Whatever the reasons may be, it is quite evident that the "no lathe" sentiment is growing. For example, the *American Watchmakers Institute News* of May 1975 carried an article on this question. Again, as a result of this new look, the horologists' trade magazines carry more advertising slanted to specialized services. For example one advertisement reads: "Barrels, wheels, pinions and pivoting. Send samples for estimate." Another advertisement reads: "Wheel cutting and antique repairs." It follows that the average horologist does not do as many jobs as he used to do. While there are some who hold that it is possible to tackle such jobs in a variety of hand operations, in my own training and experience I have found no substitute for the lathe. Yet, I am willing to admit that in today's horological practice, there are fewer occasions to use the lathe.

So, accept things as they are today and send that particular job to those who specialize in that kind of service.

 # THE GRANDFATHER CLOCK

With regard to the service of grandfather clocks, it is usually necessary that the clock repairer make a visit to the home or apartment of the particular owner of the clock. There he will perform the following operations which are necessary in order to extricate the movement for transportation to the shop.

It is obvious that the pendulum and weights must first be removed. Following this, rotate the drums so as to wind up the cables. In most grandfather clocks, the dial and hands are secured to the movement and the complete unit can be removed from the case. Again, there are designs in which the dial is secured to the case. In these, the hands must first be removed, and following this remove the dial from the case. Now remove the movement and

FIGURE 36
American grandfather
clock by
Simon Willard,
Roxbury, Mass.,
c. 1785.

replace the hands. The hands will be needed when the clock is regulated to time.

In carrying the movement to some means of transportation, it is advisable to use a large cardboard box lined with a blanket to hold the movement. When the movement has finally reached the shop, we start the work with a preliminary inspection and make notes relative to the various points that are in need of correction and repair. It is better to be aware of errors at this stage than to find them after the clock has been cleaned, repaired and assembled.

CHECKING THE STRIKING MECHANISM

If the hands and dial are attached to the movement, remove the hands and dial. Then replace the minute hand. Move the minute hand slowly and check the striking. Now is the time to check for marks on the wheel and pinion which perform the function of locking and warning. If there are none, mark with a sharp instrument the points where the wheel gears with the pinion. If this is done, the striking mechanism may be dismantled and reassembled by noting the marks, and the striking action will remain correct—that is, of course, if it was correct before dismantling.

CHECKING THE ESCAPEMENT

Observe the lock of the escape-wheel teeth on the pallets. This is done by moving the crutch to the right and thereby allowing a tooth of the escape wheel to lock on the receiving pallet. Now move the crutch to the left so that a tooth of the escape wheel will lock on the discharging pallet.

The locking may call for adjustment. If the locking is deep, the pendulum will need a wide angle of swing. This will require more power to impel the pendulum. If the locking is shallow, mislocking is possible, resulting in an erratic time rating.

Pallets in most grandfather clocks are provided with a means of adjustment. Sometimes, however, the difficulty may be worn holes in the pieces that support the escape-wheel arbor. If this is the case, bushings will need to be fitted.

CHECKING WORN PARTS

Referring to our notes, it is decided that *a*) the job needs bushings for a number of train wheels, *b*) the pivots of the wheel arbors are worn and need reducing and polishing, and *c*) the locking on the pallets needs reducing to provide a good escapement action.

The movement is now dismantled and the above problems are given the proper attention and the necessary work. The methods of repair are covered in Chapter 6.

CLEANING THE MOVEMENT

The cleaning of the movement now follows, and the procedure for cleaning is also covered in Chapter 6.

After the cleaning and assembly, the movement is tested for correct striking and then placed on a shelf having holes for the pendulum and weights.

ADJUSTING THE BEAT

Probably the best way to adjust the beat is to observe the swinging of the crutch. Having made certain that the clock is standing in a level position, we start testing the beat in the following manner: Hold the crutch between the thumb and first finger and move the crutch to the left and stop at the moment when a tooth of the escape wheel drops off a pallet. Note the distance between the crutch and the line of centers.

Now move the crutch to the right and stop at the time when a tooth of the escape wheel drops off the opposite pallet. If the left and right swings of the crutch are equal from the line of centers, the escapement is in beat. If the distances are not equal, the beat error will show. The correction consists in bending the crutch away from the side that has the longest swing.

Further observation should include fitting the pendulum bob and listening to the *tick* and the *tock*. The sounds should be equally spaced. If they are not, further adjustment of the crutch is called for.

MOON DISK

Many grandfather clocks have what is called the *moon phase*. Painted on the moon disk are two moons and this disk revolves once in two months. The opening, indicating the moon phase, is large enough to show only one moon for any given period.

The gearing system operating the moon disk has its beginning with the hour wheel of the dial train. In most grandfather clocks the moon disk has 58 teeth. The last wheel on the train pushes the moon disk one tooth each day and this agrees very closely with the actual moon phases seen on most calendars.

There are, however, other designs in which the gear ratios differ. One such design moves the moon disk one tooth every 12 hours, and in this design the moon disk has 116 teeth.

THE PORTABLE CLOCK

A portable clock obviously cannot use a pendulum. In these clocks the timing unit is the balance wheel and the hairspring. Furthermore, the escapement must dispense with the crutch and have in its place a piece called the *pallet fork*. Figure 37 shows the club-tooth escapement, a type used in high-grade portable clocks. Also shown are the names of the various parts. Figure 38 shows the pin-lever escapement, a type used in alarm clocks and popular-priced wall clocks.

Figures 39 and 40 show the balance wheels used with the above escapements. Since there are many styles of clocks using the balance and hairspring, it follows that the clock repairer must be prepared to include the portable clocks in his general benchwork. As a typical example we

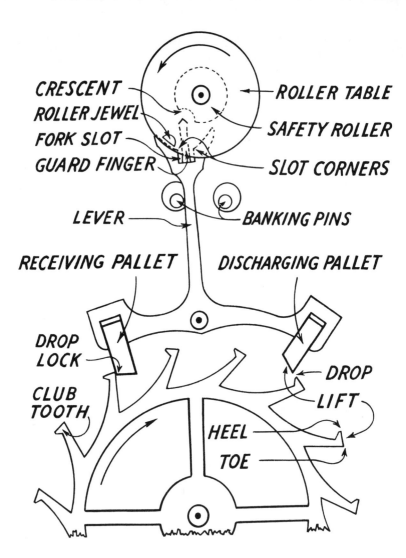

FIGURE 37
The club-tooth lever escapement.

will consider the cleaning, repair and adjustment of a portable clock with a club-tooth escapement. Its modern design is seen in Figure 41. Figure 42 shows a clock fitted with a balance similar to the one illustrated in Figure 43.

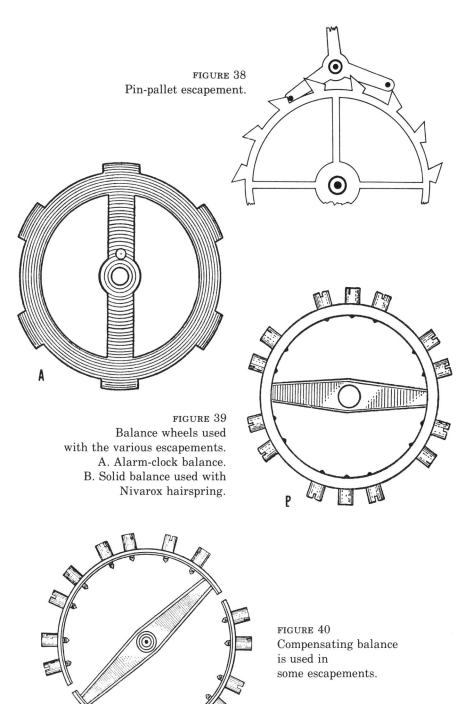

FIGURE 38
Pin-pallet escapement.

A

FIGURE 39
Balance wheels used
with the various escapements.
A. Alarm-clock balance.
B. Solid balance used with
Nivarox hairspring.

B

FIGURE 40
Compensating balance
is used in
some escapements.

C

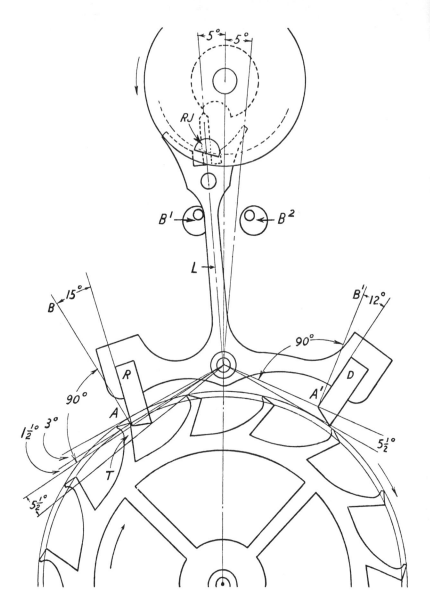

FIGURE 41
Lever escapement with slide added.

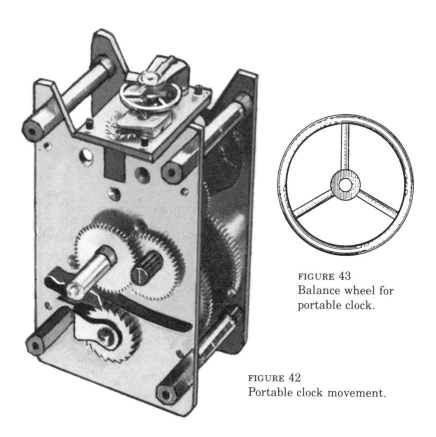

FIGURE 43
Balance wheel for
portable clock.

FIGURE 42
Portable clock movement.

CLEANING AND OILING

After removing the movement from the case the next procedure is to remove the balance assembly. Release the hairspring from the balance bridge and place the balance on an anvil. These parts will require special handling in the cleaning process, to be discussed later. Now let the mainspring down and, following this, remove the pallet fork. Then proceed with the general dismantling. This includes removing the cap jewels from the lower plate and from the balance bridge. It is important, too, to remove the mainspring from the barrel, for it is often found that the mainspring is set. It is true that the new alloyed mainsprings do not lose their elasticity; but, even so, it is preferable to remove the mainspring. It is not unusual to find a mainspring of incorrect width or strength.

The movement having been dismantled, we proceed with the cleaning. The method outlined in Chapter 6 is also satisfactory for portable clocks.

Assembling the movement. Replace the mainspring in the barrel. This may be done by winding in the spring with the thumb and fingers. If it is a small clock, use the mainspring winder. Next fit the barrel arbor to the barrel with pliers. Clock repairers of the old school used heavy tweezers, but that was in the days when mainsprings were made of steel. Modern clocks are supplied with a new kind of alloyed mainspring in which elasticity is greatly increased. With these, tweezers are not satisfactory, but pliers, with the jaws reshaped as shown in Figure 44, do a superior job by providing a much firmer grip on the barrel arbor. Oil the mainspring with mainspring oil. Next, fit the barrel cap with tweezers of the type shown in Figure 45. Ordinarily these tweezers are used for cutting, but by

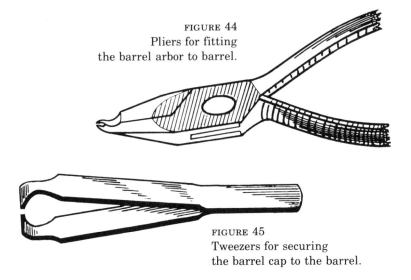

FIGURE 44
Pliers for fitting
the barrel arbor to barrel.

FIGURE 45
Tweezers for securing
the barrel cap to the barrel.

grinding the cutting edges back, leaving a flat face about one millimeter wide, and then polishing the flat face, we have tweezers unexcelled for barrel-cap replacement.

Oiling the movement. Oil the barrel arbor and fit the barrel assembly to the movement. Oil every other tooth of the escape wheel and then assemble the train wheels. Oil all of the train wheel pivots. Fit the balance-cap jewels to the plate and balance bridge and oil the jewels. Clean the balance separately in a small jar, and, after the balance has been dried, check the hairspring. If the coils of the hairspring tend to stick together, dip the balance in a cup filled with denatured alcohol or any of the special hairspring cleaners such as One Dip or the L & R hairspring cleaner. If the coils still stick after drying, repeat the treatment.

Fitting the pallet fork. Before fitting the pallet fork to the movement make certain that the tweezers are clean. Then fit the pallet fork with caution and check for freedom and end shake. The pallet-hole jewels need not be oiled.

Fitting the cannon pinion. First, oil the top end of the center-wheel post. Then, with tweezers, press the cannon pinion into position, making certain that it seats on the shoulder of the center wheel. Note that the cannon pinion is fitted before the replacement of the minute wheel and the setting wheel. If this procedure were reversed, there would be a possible chance of causing damage to the minute wheel.

Next, check the friction of the cannon pinion by pushing the leaves with the tweezers. Suppose the cannon pinion does not have the necessary friction to carry the hands. In that case, fit a V-shaped stump in the staking-tool frame. Insert a pivot broach in the cannon pinion and lay the pinion on the V-shaped stump. Select a chisel-shaped punch and give the punch a light tap with a brass hammer, thus reducing the size of the hole in the cannon pinion. Although the staking-tool method is the usual practice for closing the hole in the cannon pinion, some of the special tools shown in the tool catalogs are sometimes more convenient to use. One of these special tools recently put on the market is shown in Figure 46.

ROUTINE PROCEDURE IN ESCAPEMENT TESTING

The routine procedure in clock servicing should include a close look at the escapement. Figure 41 shows a modern design. We feel that the escapement diagnosis is passed over too lightly by many clock repairers. Comebacks due to faulty escapement action are the result. Consider now the procedure for escapement testing.

Using a 2-inch eye loupe and a clean clock oiler proceed with the first series of tests in the following order: (1) draw; (2) drop; (3) shake; (4) drop lock, and (5) slide.

DRAW

Draw is necessary to keep the guard finger from too frequent contact with the safety roller. A sudden jar will cause the lever to be thrown away from the banking and the guard finger will momentarily touch the safety roller. The draw will instantly return the lever to the banking and no particular harm is done. However, if the draw is ineffective, the guard finger will drag on the safety roller and interfere with the free motion of the balance. Stoppage sometimes results.

FIGURE 46
Cannon pinion tool.

With the mainspring partly wound, we should expect to find the lever resting against a banking. With the escapement testing tool, lift the lever away from the banking, but not so far as to unlock the pallet. Remove the tool, and the lever should, if the draw is satisfactory, return instantly to its banking. Move the lever to the opposite banking and try again. If the lever fails to return to its banking, the pallet jewels may not be clean. Sometimes the locking faces of the pallets may not be sufficiently oiled. Again, the pallet fork may not have the necessary end shake. If all the above conditions are satisfactory, want of draw could be due to improper angle of the pallet jewels.

The error such as want of draw is extremely rare in the modern clock. Improved manufacturing techniques are, no doubt, responsible. However, the older clocks of the kind usually regarded as antiques occasionally have this error. When want of draw is the problem, the corrective procedure is as follows: Remove the pallet fork from the movement and secure the fork, upside down, on the pallet jewel setter. Add small bits of jewel cement to the jewels and hold the tool over the alcohol lamp until the cement melts. Next, press on the pallet wanting in draw in such a way as to increase the angle. Sometimes the jewel fits so tightly in the slot that tilting is impossible. In that case, widen the slot or fit a narrower pallet jewel.

DROP

With a tooth locked on the receiving pallet, observe the space that separates the letting-off corner of the discharging pallet from the heel of the tooth. Now move the lever to the opposite banking pin, thereby causing the tooth on the receiving pallet to drop off the pallet and another tooth to lock on the discharging pallet. Next, observe the space that separates the letting-off corner of the receiving pallet from the heel of the tooth. Obviously, the drops should be equal, but we do not always find it so; and again, as stated above, the problem is related particularly to antiques.

A small drop on the receiving pallet is called *close outside,* and the correction consists in bringing the pallets closer together. Again, if the drop is small on the discharging pallet, the condition is termed *close inside,* and the correction consists in spreading the pallets. After altering the drops, recheck the draw.

SHAKE

When moving the lever away from the bankings (but not far enough to unlock a pallet), the space separating a pallet and tooth is less than that shown by the drop. This space is called *shake* and the presence of this phenomenon shows clearly why an adequate drop is necessary.

DROP LOCK

The usual practice in testing for drop lock is to slowly move the lever until a tooth drops off a pallet. The lock on the opposite pallet is the *drop lock.* At the moment of drop lock, it will be observed that the lever does not touch the banking. Additional motion is required for the lever to reach the banking and this additional motion is called *slide.* Drop lock plus slide is called *total lock.* Obviously the test should be made on both pallets. An approximate measure for total lock is seen when the total lock equals $1/6$ of the width of the pallet jewels.

As noted above, the motion of the lever to the banking after drop lock indicates the presence of slide. There is, however, a better method of testing for slide. The proce-

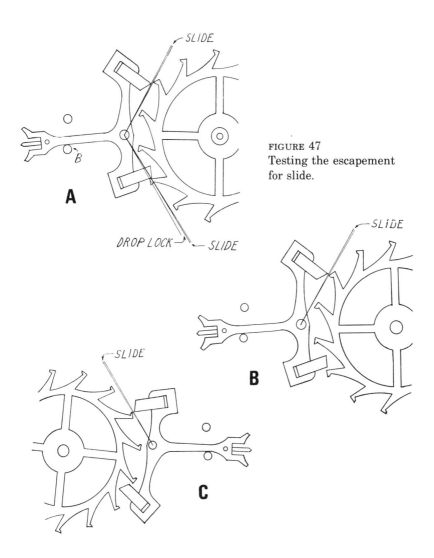

FIGURE 47
Testing the escapement
for slide.

dure is as follows: Hold the movement in such a position that the pallet fork is horizontal (see Figure 47A) with the lever dropped to the banking pin B. Gravity will hold the lever to the banking as the testing continues. With a clean clock oiler, back up the escape wheel just enough to line up the tooth and pallet as shown in Figure 47B. A movement undergoing direct examination should show a relative space between the tooth and pallet. In other words, visible space must be definitely observed and in no case should the clearance be so small as to be barely discernible. Now turn the movement halfway around and repeat the test on the opposite pallet as shown in Figure 47C.

FITTING THE BALANCE ASSEMBLY

The next procedure is to insert the hairspring stud in the balance bridge, tighten the stud screw, and adjust the regulator pins. Following this, carefully turn the balance and bridge unit over and fit it to the lower plate of the movement. Note the balance end shake and make corrections if needed.

Suppose the end shake is too great. In this case, using a graver, place a scratch mark on the lower plate in an area that would cause the end of the balance bridge carrying the balance jewels to tip downward slightly. Then, when the balance bridge is replaced in position, the end shake will be shown to be reduced.

If there is a need for additional end shake, the scratch mark is placed on the opposite area—that is, toward the balance. The balance jewel area of the balance bridge will then be raised.

CHECKING THE BALANCE ARC OF MOTION

The balance arc of motion should be 540 degrees. But how can we determine the proper balance arc of motion? This can be done by using the following method: The balance is at rest—that is, there is no tension on the hairspring. Now rotate the balance 180 degrees and stop. Release the balance and the force of the hairspring will cause the balance to return to its point of rest and the escapement action will carry it 180 degrees farther. This gives the balance a motion of 360 degrees. Now rotate the balance 270 degrees and allow it to return to its point of rest and as far on the opposite side. The balance arc of motion is now 540 degrees and the balance will continue to vibrate between these points as long as the proper motive power is maintained. The arms of the balance become visible at the moment the balance completes the arc and starts in the opposite direction. It is, therefore, at the time the balance stops that the distance covered can be determined.

If the balance arc of motion is too short, the difficulty is related to the mainspring, which could be set or too weak. In either case a new mainspring should be fitted.

If the balance arc of motion is too long, fit a mainspring of less strength.

ADDITIONAL ESCAPEMENT TESTS

Two tests are routine and these are (1) guard safety test, and (2) the corner safety test.

GUARD SAFETY TEST

Rotate the balance so that the roller jewel stands outside the fork slot, and with the first finger hold the balance in this position. Now, with a clean clock oiler, lift the lever away from the banking, thereby causing the guard finger to come into contact with the edge of the safety roller as shown in Figure 48. With the lever held in this position, examine the remaining lock on the pallet. This remaining lock is called *safety lock* and it should show a lock equal to one half of drop lock or ¾ degree of lock. The test should next be tried on the opposite pallet and a similar lock should be observed.

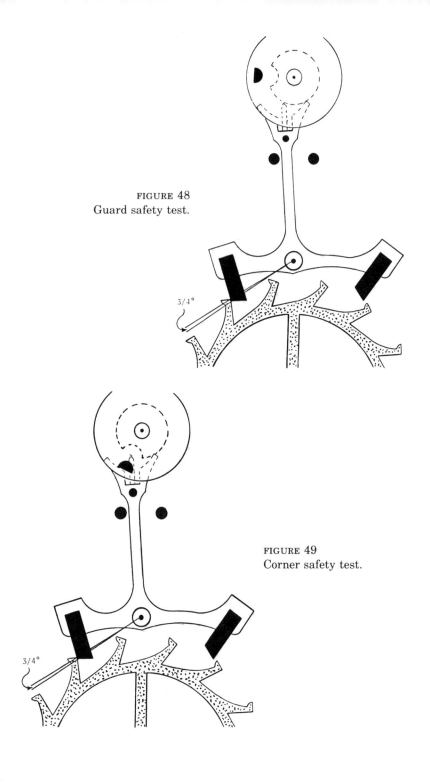

FIGURE 48
Guard safety test.

3/4°

FIGURE 49
Corner safety test.

3/4°

CORNER SAFETY TEST

Starting with the roller jewel in the fork slot, rotate the balance slowly and stop at the moment when one tooth of the escape wheel passes the letting-off corner of a pallet and another tooth locks on the opposite pallet. A slight additional turn applied to the balance will bring the roller jewel to a position opposite the slot corner. With the balance held in this position, lift the lever away from the banking, thereby causing the slot corner to come into contact with the roller jewel as shown in Figure 49. With the lever held in this position, examine the remaining, or safety, lock. Try this test on the opposite pallet, and if the safety lock is the same on both pallets the lever's angular motion from the line of centers is practically equal.

The above analysis of the cleaning, checking and repairing of the portable clock movement covers what may be called the usual procedure and with no unusual problems evident. Every clock repairer knows that many jobs are just not this simple and that additional repairs may be required in many cases. With regard to those clocks that evidence the need for repairs less frequently encountered, we will consider the repair suggestions outlined in this next section.

THE BALANCE PIVOTS

First, let us take a look at the balance pivots. The pivots should be cylindrical and the balance-hole jewels

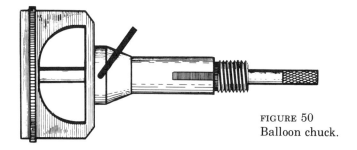

FIGURE 50
Balloon chuck.

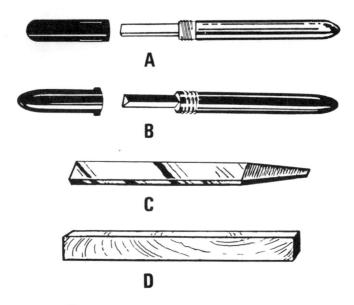

FIGURE 51
Tools used for repairing and polishing balance staff pivots.
A. Arkansas slip.
B. Jasper slip.
C. Steel burnisher.
D. Boxwood slip.

should fit freely all the way to the cone and with a slight tip so as to provide the necessary side shake.

For the repair and polishing of the balance pivots, we suggest the use of the balloon chuck (an attachment used in the lathe) shown in Figure 50. Three sizes are available. Pivots with grooves resulting from ordinary wear may be restored to a satisfactory condition by using the four tools shown in Figure 51. First apply the Arkansas slip. For further smoothing of the work use the jasper slip. Next, use the steel burnisher, and finally polish with the boxwood slip and diamantine. If the pivots are only slightly corroded, begin work with the jasper slip and continue with the steel burnisher and finally with the boxwood slip and diamantine.

If a pivot is slightly bent, straightening and restoring the pivot to satisfactory condition is often possible. Heat the pivot-straightening tweezers over the alcohol lamp and apply the heated jaws to the bent pivot. This procedure tempers the pivot slightly and breakage is less likely. Then straighten the pivot, keeping careful check on your progress by using a high-powered eye loupe. If the pivot has a satisfactory polish, no further treatment is required.

TRUING HAIRSPRINGS

The condition of the hairspring can be one reason why a clock fails to function properly. Suppose the hairspring in a given clock has a wobble around the collet. Place the balance in the hairspring truing calipers and turn the balance slowly. Using a 2-inch eye loupe observe the innermost coil around the collet. For convenience in describing the errors present in the hairspring, the usual method is to divide the first coil into quarters. Thus we have a pinning point, first quarter, half, and third quarter. The hairspring may be wide at any of these points. Again, the hairspring may be high or low at the half.

Our example is out of true in both the flat and the round. The flat should be corrected first. Stop the balance with the first finger so as to determine the high or low point in relation to the pinning point. If high at the half, press downward with a small screwdriver at a point slightly beyond the first quarter. If low at the half, insert the blade of a small screwdriver under the hairspring so that the blade rests on the arm of the balance near the half. Now turn the screwdriver in such a manner that the blade acts as a wedge between the balance arm and the coil at the half. This procedure will raise the low section and with much less chance of accident as compared with a strict lifting action.

After truing the flat examine the round. Note the point where the inner coil jumps outward or inward from the collet. Next, note the relation of the jump to the pinning point. In truing the round practically all corrections of the hairspring are done within the first quarter coil around the collet.

Three examples are shown in Figure 52. In each case, the hairsprings at *A* show the errors. The arrows show the manner in which the errors are corrected and *B* in each case shows the corrected hairspring. Usually a twisting motion with the tweezers is all that is required. In a few cases, a push or a pull with a small pointed instrument will do the work. Others cases may require manipulations at two or more points.

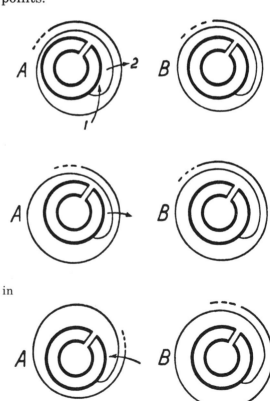

FIGURE 52
Correcting errors in
the hairspring.

If the condition of the hairspring is beyond repair, a new hairspring may be obtained from a tool and material dealer. All material dealers have either a department or a connection where a new hairspring may be timed to the required vibrations. You will need to take or send to the material dealer, the balance wheel, the old hairspring, and the balance bridge, together with the make and model number of your clock.

ESCAPEMENT PROBLEMS

Insufficient slide. A common functional error that shows an erratic rate is the want of an adequate amount of slide. The adjustment consists in slightly opening the banking on the side in need of slide.

There are, however, a few cases in which the opening of a banking or both bankings is not the proper procedure. Suppose the drop lock is rather deep. In a problem of this type you must reduce the lock. As a guide in determining which pallet jewel is to be altered, note which side shows the greater amount of guard and corner freedom. The pallet jewel on the opposite side is the one to be pushed in. It will be seen that this correction may or may not require alteration of the banking pins.

Tripping error. Periodic stopping of a clock can be caused by a functional failure termed a *tripping error.* It is that condition wherein a pallet jewel unlocks a tooth when the guard and corner safety tests are applied. Two distinct types of difficulties are possible when this error is noted. The most likely error is that of a light drop lock. To clarify this point, suppose a particular clock is of the type supplied with adjustable banking pins. In banking to the drop, the roller jewel either will not leave the fork slot or, if the escapement is out of angle, the roller jewel may leave the fork slot only on one side. The correction consists in advancing the pallet jewel on the side where the lever's angular motion is longer from the line of centers.

Adjusting the fork slot to the correct height. Another problem that is often overlooked, yet especially important, is the need to raise the lever in order to align the fork slot to the roller table. To bend the lever as needed, place the lever top-side up, on an ordinary eraser and note the point where the guard finger and the pallet arbor touch the eraser. Make two holes in the eraser at these points, replace the lever and rub carefully with the tweezers, checking your progress frequently, until the lever has been bent enough to align the fork slot properly.

Excessive guard freedom. In this example, the guard freedom was greater than the corner freedom. The drop locks were satisfactory and likewise the corner-safety test. The diagnosis suggested that everything was satisfactory except the condition of the guard finger. It was too short and too narrow. The correction consisted in flattening the end of the guard finger. This can often be done with the pivot straightening tweezers. If the guard finger is made of a hard metal that resists flattening in this manner, you should use the staking tool. With a suitable stump and punch and by applying a light tap with the brass hammer, the guard finger can be satisfactorily flattened. After flattening the end of the guard finger, it is usually necessary to correct the sides of the flattened end with the Arkansas slip. Making the flattened end V-shaped provides the needed guard freedom and safety lock.

ERRORS IN THE MAIN TRAIN

If the balance assembly and the escapement diagnosis and correction does not appear to be the answer in solving difficulties in the problem clock, consider next the possibility of excessive side shake in any of the train wheels due to normal wear. This condition can create a depthing error between a wheel and pinion, resulting in a loss of power and a balance motion much too short. The correction consists in closing holes or the fitting of new jewels with correct hole sizes.

Closing holes. If the holes in a seven-jewel movement are not too badly worn, the closing of holes can be done with the staking tool. Select a flat-faced stump that fits in the recess of the plate or bridge and place it in the die of the staking-tool frame. Using a round-end punch that fits the oil cup, tap the hole just enough so that the pivot will not go in. Then broach out the hole until the pivot fits freely. Next, fit the wheel between the plate and bridge and observe the end shake. Suppose the end shake is too great. If the movement is fitted with friction bushings, these can be shifted to the location required. If the plate and bridges are not fitted with bushings, a practical method of altering excessive end shake is to make or remodel a stump by turning a slight hollow on its face. When the hole is closed as described above, the metal in the plate or bridge will sink into the hollow of the stump, thereby decreasing the end shake. If the end shake is wanting, use a stump with a slightly convex face.

Often the holes for the escape wheel and pallet fork are found to be worn beyond repair. Since the clock repairer of today can take advantage of friction jeweling, it is a simple matter to broach out the holes to the required size and push friction jewels in place.

THE ENGLISH REGULATOR CLOCK

In Figure 1 at the beginning of this book we show the movement of the American regulator clock. Since the regulator clocks of European manufacture differ quite widely from the American design, it seems desirable that we should add a short chapter here dealing with the English regulator clock.

The English regulator clock has a pendulum beating seconds and the type of pendulum is the gridiron compensating design. This is to be seen in the lower area of the case shown in Figure 54. The clock is weight driven and is equipped with a Graham dead-beat escapement.

Removing the movement. In removing the movement from the case, first back out the two finger screws located underneath the movement as shown in Figure 53. Then slide

FIGURE 53

English regulator clock movement.

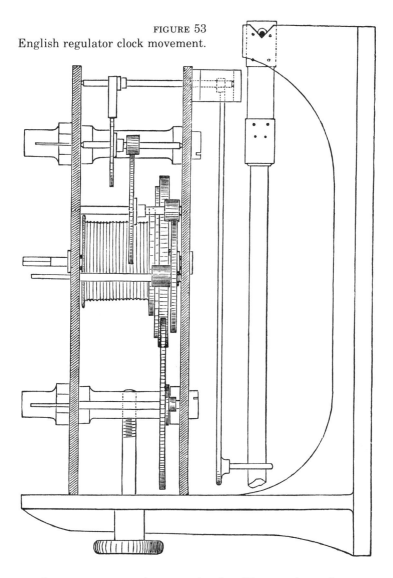

out the movement. As seen in the illustration, the pendulum remains in the back of the case. The pendulum is removed and replaced separately from the movement.

The dismantling and cleaning procedure does not differ materially from that described in Chapter 6. See that section for complete instructions.

One rather exclusive feature found in most European regulators is the planning of the dial. This can be seen in Figure 54. The hand at the bottom of the dial indicates the hours; the long hand in the middle indicates the minutes, and the hand near the top indicates the seconds. The argument presented to justify the three is that this arrangement assists in obtaining a very accurate reading of the time.

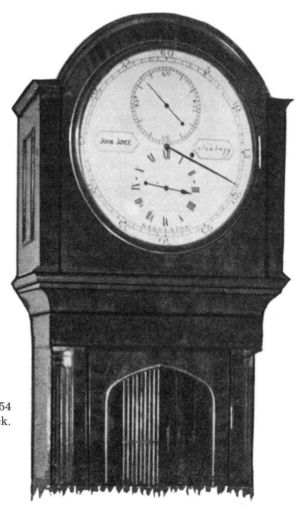

FIGURE 54
English regulator clock.

Why the regulator clock? The clock termed *regulator* is a timepiece that served special purposes many years ago. Clock and watch repairers of the old school used the regulator clock for the testing and regulating of the clocks and watches brought in for repair. Because the prime requirement of such a clock was accuracy, it generally was not equipped with a strike mechanism, so even that slight interference with timekeeping efficiency was eliminated. Usually the regulator clock was fitted with a temperature-compensated seconds pendulum and a dead-beat escapement. Its rugged movement was manufactured to the highest standards of clock making.

In years past the regulator clock was to be seen in the windows of many jewelry stores. Precision timepieces of exceptional quality, still called regulators, were found in observatories and served the purpose of broadcasting the correct time in a particular area. Today, all this has changed. Electronic timekeepers now do the job. A cesium beam atomic clock now operating at the National Bureau of Standards has a potential accuracy of one part in ten billion, which is equal to an error of one second in 300 years. Basically it is a precision quartz clock with a frequency of vibration attaining 9,192,632 cycles per second. This is the type of clock that now gives us the time we live by.

The regulator clock may now be considered obsolete, but there are still many regulator clocks in stores, offices, schools and homes. So the clock repairer will continue for many years to service this historic timepiece. It is worth noting, however, that in past years the temptation was great to capitalize on the well-deserved reputation of the regulator clock. And therefore not every clock carrying the designation of "regulator" really has the timekeeping characteristics to make it worthy of the name.

THE AMERICAN ALARM CLOCK

10

Clock repairers generally do not like to work on popular-priced alarm clocks. Owing to the low cost of the clock, it is not practical to go into extensive repairs. There are a few repairs, however, that should be pointed out. In most of these cases, the popular-priced alarm clock can be restored to good running order at a minimum cost in time and labor. Remember, also, that the older models have begun to qualify as antiques. One of them is shown in Figure 55.

Dismantling the clock. The first action should be to remove the time-winding and alarm-winding keys that are located on the back of the clock. Arrows indicate the direction in which the keys are to be turned to wind. To remove them, simply turn the keys in the opposite direction, as most of these keys are screwed on. In a few cases, however,

FIGURE 55
Antique alarm clock.

the keys are fitted friction tight to a square on the arbor. If this is the present case, insert the jaws of your cutting pliers under the keys and pry them off. Usually the movement may be removed from the case without disturbing the time-setting and alarm-setting knobs, as the holes in the back plate are large enough to permit the knobs to go through. Removing the movement from the case differs, however, according to the make of the clock. A quick examination should determine this. In most alarm clocks the bezel is pried off and three or four screws at the back are removed. The movement is then lifted out for examination.

Place a mark with a needle file or watch screwdriver on the outer coil of the hairspring at the point where the hairspring is secured to the stud. Remove the brass wedge to release the hairspring. With your pliers back out one of the threaded steel cups that carry the balance wheel and remove the balance assembly from the movement.

Examine the pivots of the balance staff. The ends of the pivots should feel sharp when touched with the finger. If, due to wear, they are not sharp to the touch, they must be made so. Place the staff in a split chuck and grind the pivots to a sharp point with an Arkansas slip. Finish with a steel burnisher.

Cleaning the movement. With the balance out of the movement, it is a simple matter to clean the movement, but first remove the hands and dial. The ultrasonic watch-cleaning solution is satisfactory for cleaning. Place enough solution in a jar to cover the movement and then place the movement in the jar. Dip a cleaning brush in the solution and scrub the movement thoroughly, particularly around the pivot holes and the circumference of the escape wheel. After cleaning, rinse the movement in the ultrasonic rinsing solution and then dry the movement under a heating lamp. Following this, give the balance a similar treatment.

After the parts are dry, replace the balance in the movement. The mark previously made on the hairspring shows the proper position. Adjust the threaded steel cups to permit a small freedom for the staff end-shake.

Oiling the movement is next in order. Wind the time and alarm mainsprings, and place mainspring oil on the coils. Oil the train wheel pivots, the balance pivots and every other tooth of the escape wheel, also the alarm-wheel teeth.

The balance should now start with a full motion of not less than 450 degrees. If it does not, we must look for additional problems.

Adjusting the escapement. If the balance does not take a satisfactory motion, the escapement may be at fault. Turn the balance slowly until such time as to allow one tooth to pass a pallet pin. The escape wheel will turn and another tooth will engage the opposite pallet pin. There should be a definite locking as shown in Figure 39. At this point we may find an error wherein the pallet pin fails to lock, and if this is the case, the pallet pin will engage the impulse face of the tooth. Using long, flat-nosed pliers, we make the correction by bending toward the escape wheel arbor the narrow projection of brass in which the pivot of the pallet arbor is fitted. Bending the pallet arbor tongue puts the pallet fork slightly out of upright, since the opposite end usually has no such means of adjustment. This, however, is not objectionable in clocks of this quality. The only additional adjustment is bending the lever to line up the fork slot to the impulse pin.

Fitting pallet pins. If the pallet pins are worn, new pins should be fitted. Let the mainspring down and remove the pallet fork from the movement. Since the pins are fitted in place by friction, it is only necessary to lay the pallet fork on the anvil and drive out the pins. Ordinary sewing needles of correct diameter are well adapted to serve as new pins. Cut the needles to the required length, finish the ends and drive them into place. Since the needles are highly polished, no further finishing is necessary.

Adjusting the alarm. On the dial side of the movement lies a long flat spring with a bent-over end that reaches through a hole in the plate. The bent-over end locks or releases a lever which permits the alarm to function at the desired time. When turning the alarm-setting knob, one can readily see what happens and the necessary adjustment can be made. So the clock repairer should have no problem with this when he has an alarm clock on the bench in front of him.

Replacing the hands. Turn the alarm-setting knob slowly and stop the instant the clock alarms. Fit the alarm indicator hand to 12 o'clock. Fit the hour and minute hands to 12 o'clock also. Next, turn the time-setting knob forward clockwise, and check the time when the clock alarms. If the alarm does not take place at 12 o'clock, readjust the hands until the clock alarms at the proper time.

THE
400-DAY
CLOCK

Instead of using the conventional pendulum, the 400-day clock has the equivalent of a balance suspended at the end of a flattened wire. This is generally referred to as the *torsion pendulum* and is shown in Figure 56.

Designed as it is to run a year between windings, it will be noted (see Figure 57) that there are three intermediate wheels. The barrel makes one turn in 80 days and the balance makes 8 vibrations a minute or 7½ seconds for each vibration. Exceptions may be found in some of the older models.

The escapement is of the dead-beat type. Some models are made with adjustable pallets as shown in Figure 58A; while other manufacturers use pallets of one-piece construction.

Lying above the pallet frame is a round wire about 1½ inches long called the *pallet pin,* the upper end of which plays freely in the slot of the fork F as shown in Figure 58B. The fork is secured to the suspension spring S. When the impulse is delivered to the fork, the suspension spring is twisted and the force is carried to the torsion pendulum.

REPAIRING THE 400-DAY CLOCK

The general analysis of cleaning clock movements given in Chapter 6 applies also to the 400-day clock, but the adjustment of the escapement, the fitting of a new suspension spring, and the correcting of the beat present

FIGURE 56
The 400-day clock
movement.

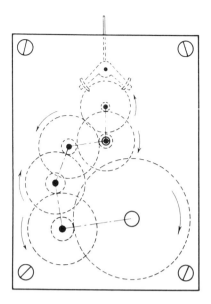

FIGURE 57
400-day clock.
A. Escapement
B. Impulse assembly

new problems. Readjusting of the pallets is rarely needed, but the correction of errors relative to the fork and pallets call for comment.

Adjusting the beat. Assume that the clock is set up and running. This is the time to check the beat. Listen to the tick. The balance will continue its circular arc of motion after the tick, and the lock on the pallets will become deeper. This additional lock is called *run* and should be equal on both pallets. This may be noted by observing the distance covered by the torsion pendulum after the tick. If it is equal for both clockwise and counterclockwise motions, the escapement is in beat.

If this additional motion is not equal, it may be made so by turning the block *B* that supports the upper end of the suspension spring. This piece is called the *beat adjust-*

er block and usually is fitted friction tight in the plate *P* (see Figure 57B). In some models, other designs are used. One frequently seen model has a set screw that must be loosened to permit the turning of the beat adjuster block. Before adjusting the block, however, it is well to inspect the suspension spring for bends or kinks that may lie above the fork. If the suspension spring appears to be in good condition, the beat error is corrected by turning the beat adjuster block in the direction that will bring the fork

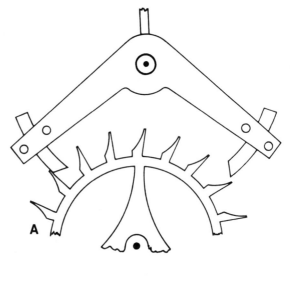

A

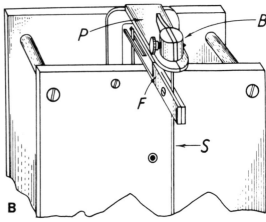

FIGURE 58
The 400-day clock,
showing the
torsion pendulum.

B

toward the side where the balance motion after the tick is shorter.

Fitting a suspension spring. Suppose a clock for repair has a broken suspension spring. This may be obtained from a tool and material dealer by sending in the old spring as a sample. In fitting a new spring, first determine the required length. Then fit the end pieces and the fork. Secure the torsion pendulum assembly to the movement and set up the clock for running. Check the beat and regulate to time.

Fluttering. Often, after fitting a new suspension spring, a malfunction called *fluttering* may be observed. This is a condition wherein the pallets receive and discharge several teeth of the escape wheel in the same time that the torsion pendulum makes one turn. The clock may gain several hours in, say, one half hour. Fluttering can be eliminated by raising the fork on the suspension spring. This adjustment also tends to increase the torsion pendulum arc of motion.

Torsion pendulum motion. The pendulum arc of motion should be approximately 360 degrees for a single vibration. A shorter motion is permissible provided the run is adequate. A run that terminates too close to the tick could result in stopping. The run can sometimes be increased by bending the pallet pin toward the suspension spring or, as noted above, by raising the fork on the suspension spring.

THE CHRONOMETER

The development of the chronometer had its beginning with the work of John Harrison (1693–1776). The Board of Longitude, an English organization, offered a prize of £20,000 for the creation of an instrument that would determine longitude at sea within certain limits. Harrison's first timepiece (shown in Figure 59) failed to meet the needed requirements, but timepiece Number Four (see Figure 60) did the job and he was paid the £20,000. Harrison's timepiece (the term *chronometer* was not used at this time) was not built on the principles of the modern chronometer. But his work was followed by several men who built real chronometers. The best among these early chronometer makers were Pierre LeRoy, F. Berthoud, John Arnold, and Thomas Earnshaw.

These early chronometers used the cylindrical

FIGURE 59
John Harrison's No. 1 timepiece.

hairspring shown in Figure 61A and the compensating balance shown in Figure 61B. The mechanical principles of today's chronometer escapement were developed by Thomas Earnshaw (1749–1829). Its construction and action will now be considered.

ESCAPEMENT

Construction. The escape wheel is of brass and for lightness the arms are reduced to half the thickness of the teeth. The locking of the teeth is inclined about 30 degrees to facilitate the draw. The diameter of the steel impulse roller *IR* is one half that of the escape wheel and is planted between two teeth of the escape wheel. Theoretically the impulse roller intersects a path of 24 degrees measured from the escape-wheel center. Actually the circular path is less, allowing for the necessary clearance. Accordingly the balance arc is slightly less than 45 degrees.

The discharging roller *DR* and the pallet *DP* lie below the impulse roller *IR* The discharging pallet engages the gold spring *GS* of the detent. The size of the discharging

FIGURE 60
Harrison's No. 4 timepiece won prize.

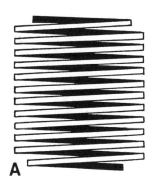
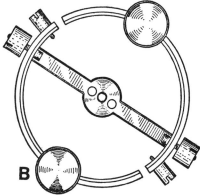

FIGURE 61
Hairspring and balance used in early chronometers.
A. Cylindrical hairspring
B. Compensating balance

roller is important if the detent is to return on time to lock the escape wheel.

The detent is a length of hardened and tempered steel whose parts are shown in the illustration and indicated as follows: *F*, the foot; *S*, the spring; *B*, the blade, and *H*, the horn. A hole is bored in the blade to receive the locking pallet *LP*. Screwed to the blade and projecting beyond is the gold spring *GS*.

Action of the escapement. The balance is rotating in the direction of the arrow. Likewise the discharging pallet *DP* turns and pushes the detent to the right. This action releases the escape-wheel tooth from the locking pallet *LP*. The escape wheel is now free to turn in the direction of the arrow, but its free motion is retarded when tooth *A* engages the impulse pallet *IP*. The impulse pallet has already moved ahead of tooth *A* by 5 degrees, thereby securing a safe overlapping. The escape-wheel tooth now drives the impulse pallet *IP* until the divergence of their paths separates them. The instant tooth *A* drops off the impulse pallet, tooth *B* engages the locking pallet *LP*. (Return of the locking pallet took place the instant the discharging

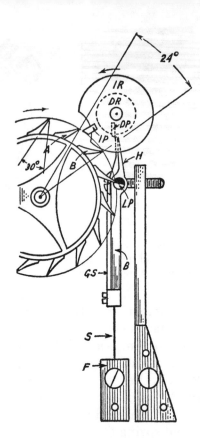

FIGURE 62
Modern chronometer
escapement.

pallet passed the gold spring.) The balance wheel continues its circular motion, winding up the hairspring until its energy is exhausted. On the return vibration, the discharging pallet *DP* pushes aside the gold spring without disturbing the detent. After the inertia of the balance is exhausted, the balance returns for another vibration precisely like the first.

Adjusting the beat. The chronometer escapement is in beat when the discharging pallet points directly toward the gold spring. In practice the hairspring is so adjusted that the gold spring just touches the discharging pallet on the side facing the escape wheel. In this position the balance may be rotated an equal distance in either direction and the escapement will start of itself.

Oiling the escapement. The chronometer escapement requires no oil, since the unlocking and impulse actions are more in the nature of a direct push with very little sliding friction. This is an advantage because the deterioration of the oil (required in other escapements) changes the rate.

Escapement error. Both the chronometer and lever escapements give most of the impulse after the line of centers, which causes the short arcs to lose. This effect can be altered in the chronometer escapement by adjusting the relative positions of the unlocking and impulse pallets. This changes the amount of drop and also the length of the

FIGURE 63
Marine chronometer.

impulse before the line of centers. It will be further observed that the hairspring can be so adjusted that there
will be no escapement error by adjusting the spring so as to
advance the impulse pallet. This seemingly desirable feature of centering the impulse is never practiced, however,
for the reason that the escapement is more apt to set.
Instead, the escapement is always put in beat as already
explained.

One point in particular should be noted here. The
balance should not be removed when the mainspring is
under tension. Either let the mainspring down completely
or lock the train by wedging a piece of cork between the
fourth wheel and the plate. The reason for this precaution
is that the locking pallet is apt to be broken off should the
train start without the balance in the movement.

PROBLEMS
TAKEN FROM
PRACTICE

This chapter consists of a compilation of seven repair and adjustment problems encountered by the writer. The purpose is to show the student reader the actual procedure in specific cases, with the hope that perhaps these examples may be the answer to difficulties you may be having with some particular job.

PROBLEM NO. 1

An 8-day pendulum shelf clock was cleaned and repaired by a student apprentice. When the clock was set up and running, it ran with reasonable accuracy for three days and then it started to lose. After seven days the clock was a half hour slow. Obviously, something was definitely wrong. Examination showed that the pallets engaged the escape wheel teeth with too much lock. The movement was so designed that the lock on the pallets could be altered. The adjustment was made and the next test showed a rate within two minutes a week without even changing the length of the pendulum.

PROBLEM NO. 2

A popular-priced grandfather clock with hour and half-hour striking movement, weight powered, and fitted with a seconds pendulum, was cleaned, and two bushings fitted. After the movement was set up on an especially designed shelf, it ran for four days and stopped.

On close examination we found that the pallets had been broken at some time and a workman had filed up a piece for one pallet and soft-soldered it to the remainder of the pallet frame. We touched the pallet with a file and found it to be rather soft. The piece was removed by first heating the soft solder; then we reheated it to a cherry red to harden it. After cleaning and polishing, the piece was soft-soldered back to the pallet frame. After the escapement was again assembled, the clock ran satisfactorily. For best performance the pallets must be glass hard. The soft pallet had apparently been the cause of the clock's stopping.

Let us suppose that a particular verge is beyond repair. In many cases a new verge can be purchased from a material dealer. It will be hardened and ready for use. Just send a sample to the dealer and give the maker and model number. Verges are also available in kits which include a number of verges of the more popular makes.

PROBLEM NO. 3

A fine French clock was cleaned. No other repairs seemed

necessary, so the movement was set up on a shelf, started and set to time. The clock kept good time while running, but it stopped after three days; seemingly without reason, for, if restarted, it would run another two days without additional winding.

Past experience suggested that the mainspring was probably set, and this proved to be the case. A new time mainspring was fitted and the clock caused no further trouble.

PROBLEM NO. 4

An American shelf clock with hour and half hour striking was cleaned. No other difficulties seemed apparent, but after setting up the clock, it ran for only three hours. When examining the movement, the difficulty appeared to be in the time train. Further checking showed a tooth of the second wheel was wedged tight in a lantern pinion. The tooth of the wheel apparently had been fitted by another clock repairer. It was loose and twisted out of shape.

The mainsprings were let down and the wheel with the tooth problem was removed from between the plates. The loose tooth was removed and the open space was filed slightly with a needle file to restore the opening to straight sides. Selecting a piece of brass of the same thickness as the wheel, the piece was filed so as to fit friction tight to the wheel. This is seen in Figure 64. The new tooth was now soldered in place with soft solder. A satisfactory method is to lay the wheel on a copper plate and hold it over an alcohol lamp until the solder melts. Following this, the tooth was filed to its proper shape with a flat needle file.

After being reassembled, the clock caused no further trouble.

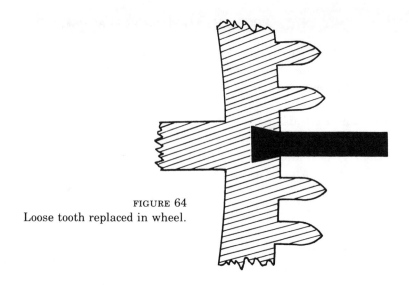

FIGURE 64
Loose tooth replaced in wheel.

PROBLEM NO. 5

This next example is a wall clock, registering time only, and lacking a pendulum. The owner explained that the clock had been in his family for two generations and the pendulum had gotten lost sometime within that period.

So the problem, in addition to cleaning and general repair, was to determine the length of the old pendulum in order to purchase a new pendulum rod with bob from a tool and material dealer.

The first procedure was to dismantle the movement and count the teeth of the wheels and leaves of the pinions. Since the second or center wheel makes one turn in an hour, we started with this wheel. Our counting indicated that the center wheel contained 100 teeth. Continuing with the counting of the remaining wheels and pinions, the main train showed the following figures:

$$\frac{100 \times 96}{8 \times 8} = 150.$$

Thus the escape wheel made 150 turns to one center

wheel turn. However, we had to know the number of vibrations the pendulum made in one hour.

The escape wheel contained 30 teeth, and since each tooth delivered two impulses to the escapement, the number used had to be doubled. Hence the number 150 (turns of the escape wheel) was multiplied by 60 and this gave us 9,000. This figure indicated the number of pendulum vibrations in one hour.

However, to apply the pendulum formula, this figure had to be reduced to the time of one vibration of the pendulum. The procedure continued as follows:

$9000 \div 60 = 150$ vibrations of pendulum per minute
$150 \div 60 = 2.5$ vibrations of pendulum per second
$1 \div 2.5 = .4$ or 2/5 second, time of one vibration

Applying the formula shown in Example 3 in Chapter 4 we proceeded as follows:

$$1^2 : 39.1 :: .4^2 : L$$

$$\frac{1}{39.1} :: \frac{.4^2}{L}$$

$$L = .16 \times 39.1$$

$$L = 6.25 \text{ inches}$$

The figure of 6.25 inches is the approximate length of the pendulum.

PROBLEM NO. 6

An American grandfather clock, powered by weights and striking the hours and half hours, had a tendency to strike very slowly in spite of the fact that the movement had been cleaned and the striking train appeared to be in good condition.

The fly has the function of regulating the speed of the striking and in this case, the only correction consisted in making the ends of the fly shorter. This was done by bending the outer end of each half of the fly back on itself. The speed of the striking was thereby increased.

Suppose we had another clock wherein the striking was too fast. In this case we would check the fly on the arbor. There might be a slipping action. Correction would call for a reshaping of the fly to create more friction.

If the friction is correct, increase the length of the fly by soft soldering thin and narrow pieces of brass to the ends of the fly. But watch carefully the amount of space in which the fly operates.

PROBLEM NO. 7

A small English clock in a brass case, commonly called a *Carriage clock,* presented an unusual problem.

The clock was fitted with a compensating balance similar to that shown in Figure 40. The clock was cleaned and the balance wheel was trued and poised. The clock then gave good service for about three months until the owner brought it back complaining that the clock had lost considerable time during the night.

The clock was tested in every conceivable way. It would run during the day and keep time. Then, the next morning, the clock would be several hours slow but still running. Further examination showed an unusual condition. The clearance between the balance screws and the underside of the balance bridge was so small that during the night, when the temperature dropped, the outward bending of the rims was sufficient to cause the screws to touch the underside of the balance bridge and thus stop the clock. During the morning hours, when the temperature rose, the clock would start of itself. The clock had been repaired in the late summer months and had run consistently then, but with the coming of cooler weather the diameter of the balance rims had become longer. The correction consisted in removing the dial washers that were fitted to the highest screws. These same washers were then fitted to the lowest screws. Now the expanding diameter of the balance rims, during the cold period, did not reach the underside of the balance bridge and the clock ran satisfactorily.

APPENDIX A
TOOLS
AND MATERIALS

In Chapter 6 mention is made of various tools and materials used by the clock repairer. These are shown in the following pages. Many other tools are included here because we are sure that these additional tools are equally useful.

Pivot file

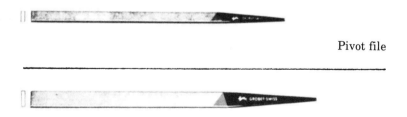

Steel burnisher

Pegwood

Pegwood knife

Pivot wire

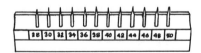

Pivot drill assortment

Needle files

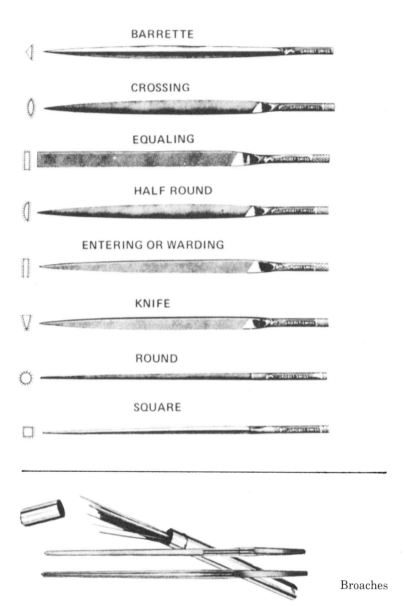

BARRETTE

CROSSING

EQUALING

HALF ROUND

ENTERING OR WARDING

KNIFE

ROUND

SQUARE

Broaches

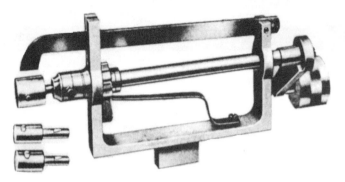

Mainspring winder

Pendulum rod with suspension
spring attached

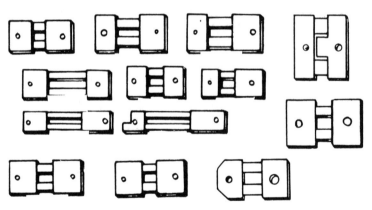

Suspension springs

Suspension steel

End cutting

Round nose

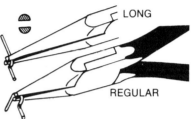

Chain nose

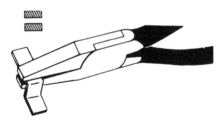

Flat nose

Diagonal cutting

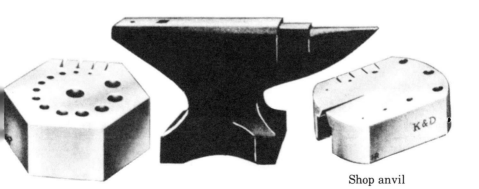

Shop anvil

Clock regulating stand

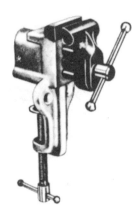

Portable vise

Bench vise

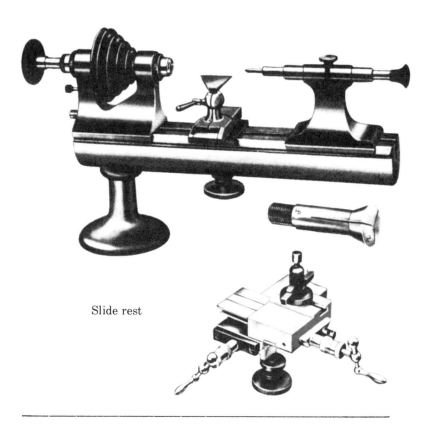

Slide rest

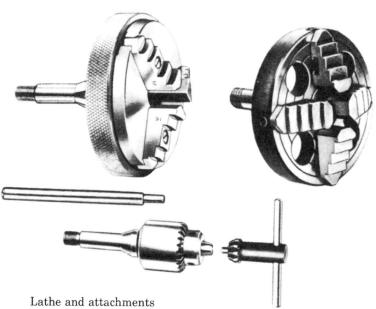

Lathe and attachments

APPENDIX B

TOOL AND
MATERIAL DEALERS

BMS Materials, *Box No. 1, Pleasantville, N.Y. 10570.*

Jules Borel and Company, *1110 Grand Avenue, Kansas City, Mo. 64106.*

Stanley Donahue, *Box No. 53149, Houston, Texas 77052.*

Friedman-Gessler Company, *315 West Fifth Street, Los Angeles, Calif. 90013.*

A. J. Goldfarb, Inc., *251 West 30th Street, New York, N.Y. 10001.*

Ralph Herman Clock House, *628 Coney Island Avenue, Brooklyn, N.Y. 11218*

The Horolovar Company, *Box No. 44A, Bronxville, N.Y. 10708*

Kilb & Company, *623 North Second Street, Milwaukee, Wis. 53203.*

S. LaRose, Inc. *Greensboro, N.C. 27420.*

Marshall-Swartchild, *2040 North Milwaukee Avenue, Chicago, Ill. 60647.*

Southwest Clock Supply, Inc. *10889 Shady Trail, Dallas, Texas, 75220.*

Tiny Clock Shop, *1354 Old Northern Blvd., Roslyn, N.Y. 11576.*

United Tool and Material Company, *307 University Building, Denver, Colo. 80202.*

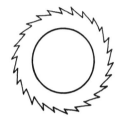 # BIBLIOGRAPHY

BOOKS

BRITTEN, F. J. *Old Clocks and Watches and Their Makers.* New York: Bonanza Books.

COWEN, HARRISON J. *Time and Its Measurement.* Cleveland: World Publishing Co.

DECARLE, DONALD. *Practical Clock Repairing.* London: N.G.A. Press.

GAZELEY, W. J. *Watch & Clock Making and Repairing.* Princeton, N.J.: D. Van Nostrand.

GOODRICH, WARD. *The Modern Clock.* Chicago: North American.

HARRIS, H. G. *Advanced Watch and Clock Repair.* New York: Emerson Books, Inc.

JONES, BERNARD E. *Clock Cleaning and Repairing.* London: Cassell & Co. Ltd.

KELLY, HAROLD C. *Clock Repairing as a Hobby.* New York: Association Press.

RAWLINGS, A. L. *The Science of Clocks and Watches.* New York: Pitman Publishing Co.

MAGAZINES

American Horologist and Jeweler, 2403 Campa Street, Denver, Colo. 80205.

Bulletin of the National Association of Watch and Clock Collectors, 335 North Third Street, Columbia, Penna. 17512.

Jewelers' Circular-Keystone, 56th and Chestnut Streets, Philadelphia, Penna. 19139.

Modern Jeweler, 1211 Walnut Street, Kansas City, Mo. 64106.

National Jeweler, 6 West 57th Street, New York, N.Y. 10019.

The Northwestern Jeweler, 142 West Main Street, Albert Lea, Minn. 56007.

Pacific Goldsmith, 657 Mission Street, San Francisco, Calif. 94105.

Southern Jeweler, 75 Third Street, N.W. Atlanta, Ga. 30308.

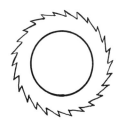 INDEX